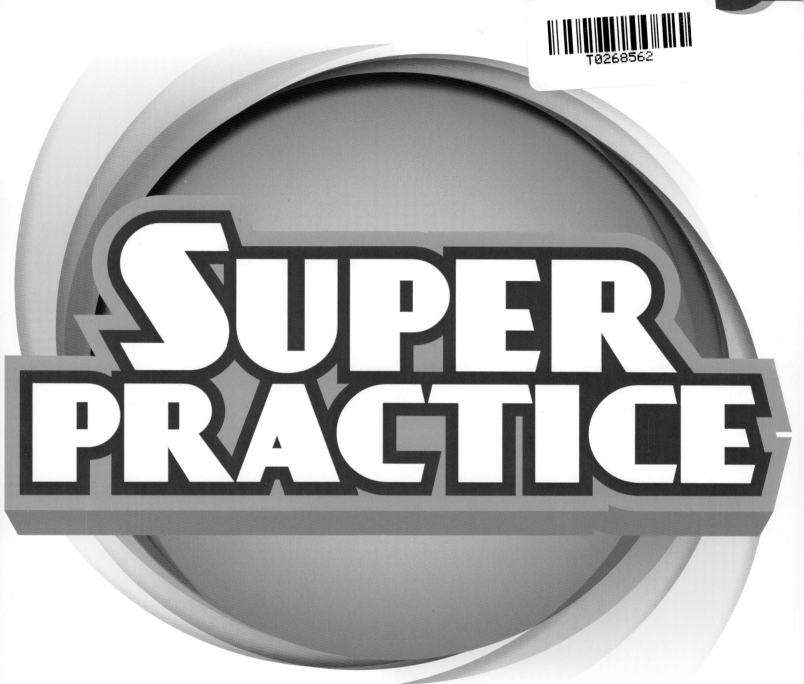

SUPER PRACTICE

Garan Holcombe

CAMBRIDGE
UNIVERSITY PRESS

Map of the Book

Unit	Grammar/Language	Reading/Writing	Listening/Speaking
(pages 4–11)	• Simple Past Review • Simple Past Questions Review	A Biography	Science and Scientists
1 (pages 12–19)	• Past Progressive Review • Two Simultaneous Actions with *While*	A Story	Natural Disasters
2 (pages 20–27)	• Numbers 100–5,000,000 • *Have to* / *Had to* Review	A Tourism Advertisement	Jungle Adventure
3 (pages 28–35)	• *Going to* Review • Time: *Past* and *To* the Hour	An Email	Music
4 (pages 36–43)	• Ordinal Numbers • Zero Conditional	An Invitation	Food in Space
5 (pages 44–51)	• *Be made of …* / *Be used for …* • Possessive Apostrophes	Classified Advertisements	Sheriffs and Robbers
6 (pages 52–59)	• *Should* / *Shouldn't* • *Could I … ?* / *Do you mind if I … ?*	A Travel Diary	Souvenirs and Vacations
7 (pages 60–67)	• *Will* for Offers and Promises • Present Perfect with *Just*	A Letter	At the Theater
8 (pages 68–75)	• First Conditional • *What if … ?*	A Newspaper Article	The Robot Exhibition
9 (pages 76–83)	• Present Perfect with *Already* and *Yet* • *Have you … yet?*	A Postcard	On Board Ship

Simple Past Review

We had a science test on Monday. It was really difficult!

Use the **simple past** to talk about something that happened in the past at a specific time.

*We **had** a science test on Monday.*

Regular verbs in the simple past are verbs that end in **ed**, such as **loved**, **used**, and **played**. They are the same for every person: **I**, **you**, **he**, **she**, **it**, **we**, **you**, **they**.

Irregular verbs in the simple past do not end in **ed**.

*My parents **went** to the supermarket and **bought** olives, apples, and yogurt.*

The simple past of **go** is **went** not **goed**. Irregular verbs in the simple past have forms that you have to learn individually, but the forms are the same for every person.

The negative is formed with **did** + **not**:

*I **didn't** go to the park. I went to the gym.*

The simple past of **be** is **was** / **were**. The negative forms are **wasn't** / **weren't**.

1 **Order the sentences to tell the story of what Burak did yesterday.**

   a He went to town to meet his friends. ☐

   b She won both games. ☐

   c He had toast for breakfast. ☐

   d In the evening, he played chess with his sister. ☐

   e They watched a movie called *The Scientist*. ☐

   f He got up early. ☐ 1

   g They had a milkshake and then went to the movies. ☐

   h It was funny. ☐

2 Write the verbs in the positive and negative form of the simple past.

1 have _____had_____ / _____didn't have_____   6 put _____ / _____
2 be _____ / _____   7 give _____ / _____
3 keep _____ / _____   8 mix _____ / _____
4 call _____ / _____   9 stay _____ / _____
5 say _____ / _____   10 watch _____ / _____

3 Complete the text. Use verbs from Activity 2.

Hi, Marta,

We **(1)** _____had_____ to do an experiment in our science class today. We **(2)** _____ on gloves and aprons. "It's very important to be safe in the labs," **(3)** _____ Mr. Torres. We also **(4)** _____ on goggles. Mr. Torres **(5)** _____ each of us a beaker— they are bigger than test tubes—and three special liquids. We **(6)** _____ the three liquids together, and then we **(7)** _____ them. The liquids **(8)** _____ the same color: they changed color from blue to white to gray to orange to blue. They **(9)** _____ changing color for a few minutes. It **(10)** _____ fantastic! It's called the Briggs–Rauscher reaction.

I think I would like to be a scientist now.

How are you, Marta?

Cesc

4 There are six mistakes in the email. The first one is given. Find, circle, and correct the other five.

Hi, Cesc,

Thanks for your email. The experiment sounds great!

We have a new chemistry teacher. Our last teacher (leaves) after a huge explosion in his laboratory. Our new teacher is named Ms. Calvo. We have our first class with her last week. It is really interesting. She tells us her ideas. She said, "Chemistry is the science of change." Then she give us some instructions for next week. Our homework is to read through them and think about them. We're going to do our first experiment in the next class!

By the way, I liked the photo you send me. You look really good in the goggles and apron!

I think I'd like to be a scientist too!

Marta

1 ___leaves___ / ___left___   3 _____ / _____   5 _____ / _____
2 _____ / _____   4 _____ / _____   6 _____ / _____

Simple Past Questions Review

> **When did** you go to bed last night?

Language Focus

Use **simple past questions** to ask someone about something that happened at a specific time in the past.

What did you do for the history of science project?

Questions and answers with simple past are formed with **did** + **infinitive** and **did** + **not** + **infinitive**.

Did you **have** a good weekend?   *Yes, I **did**. I went to my cousin's birthday party.*

The forms are the same for every person: **I**, **you**, **he**, **she**, **it**, **we**, **you**, **they**.

Question words like **why**, **when**, **where**, etc., go before **did** in the question.

Where did you go this weekend?   *We went to the theater.*

Questions with **was** / **were** are not formed with **did**. We say *Were you at home yesterday?* not ~~Did you be at home yesterday?~~ or ~~Did you was at home yesterday?~~

1 **Correct the questions.**

1 How were your science class today?

  How was your science class today?

2 Did you watched the soccer game last night?

_____

3 Where you went last Sunday?

_____

4 What present did you got for your sister's birthday?

_____

5 Was you tired this morning?

_____

6 Do you went on vacation last year?

_____

2 Complete the questions with *did*, *was*, or *were*.

1 What _____did_____ you do last weekend?

2 Where _____ you go on your last family vacation?

3 _____ you watch a movie last night?

4 What _____ the last book you read?

5 _____ you do any homework yesterday?

6 _____ all your friends at school on Monday?

3 Match the questions from Activity 2 with the answers below.

a It was *The Hobbit*. I love fantasy stories. ☐

b My friends and I played basketball in the park. It was fun. [1]

c Yes. I did two hours of science. I have a test next week. ☐

d We went to the beach. My grandparents have a house there. ☐

e No, Julio wasn't there. I think he had a cold. ☐

f No, I didn't. I played video games instead. ☐

4 Complete the questions with *what*, *when*, *where*, or *who*.

1 _____What_____ time did you get up on Saturday?

2 _____ did you have for breakfast?

3 _____ did you do that day?

4 _____ did you meet?

5 _____ did you go?

6 _____ did you come home?

5 Answer the questions from Activity 4.

1 _____

_____

2 _____

_____

3 _____

_____

4 _____

_____

5 _____

_____

6 _____

_____

Reading: A Biography

1 Read the biography. Answer the questions.

ROSALIND FRANKLIN

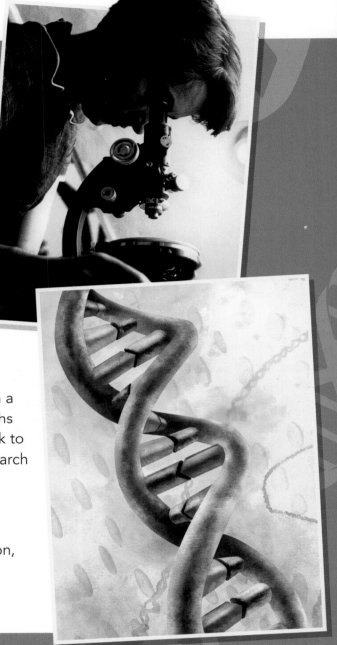

At Cambridge University in the 1950s, Francis Crick and James Watson became famous for their discovery of the structure of deoxyribonucleic acid (DNA). DNA carries the genetic information that is passed from parent to child, but Crick and Watson were not the only people who helped discover its structure.

Born in London in 1920, Rosalind Franklin studied chemistry at Cambridge University. After graduating, she worked in Paris and then moved to King's College London. It was at King's College that she began working on DNA with a scientist named Maurice Wilkins. They used X-ray photographs to study the structure of DNA. Wilkins showed Franklin's work to Crick and Watson, and they used it to help them in their research at Cambridge. In 1953, Crick and Watson published news of their discovery. It was one of the great moments of 20th-century science.

Rosalind Franklin died in 1958, four years before Crick, Watson, and Wilkins received a Nobel Prize for their discovery of the structure of DNA. It was only many years later that people recognized the importance of Franklin's work.

1 What university did Francis Crick and James Watson work at in the 1950s? ___Cambridge___

2 What subject did Franklin study in college? _____

3 Where did Franklin go after her time at Cambridge? _____

4 Who did Franklin work with at King's College London? _____

5 When did Crick and Watson tell the world about their discovery? _____

6 When did Crick, Watson, and Wilkins win their Nobel Prize? _____

Writing

1 Complete the fact file with the words and phrases in the box.

> a kind of early computer   ~~the famous poet Lord Byron~~
> London, 1815   the inventor Charles Babbage   1852   She wrote a program for it.

○ ADA LOVELACE, THE FIRST COMPUTER PROGRAMMER ○

1 Who was her father? _the famous poet Lord Byron_
2 Where and when was she born? _____
3 Who did she work with? _____
4 What did he design? _____
5 What work did she do for his invention? _____
6 When did she die? _____

Help with Writing

Biographies can help us understand other times and places. The biography of Rosalind Franklin, for example, makes us think about how hard it was for women to be recognized for their achievements. It also makes us ask whether things are different now.

2 You are going to write a biography of Ada Lovelace. Use the biography of Rosalind Franklin and the fact file in Activity 1 to help you.

A BIOGRAPHY OF ADA LOVELACE

_____
_____
_____
_____
_____
_____
_____
_____
_____
_____
_____
_____

Listening: Science and Scientists

1 🎧 **01** **Listen and number the pictures.**

2 🎧 **02** **Listen to the conversations. Circle the correct answers.**

1 What happened at school?

  a The experiment worked.

  b The experiment didn't work.

2 Where did Jill's dad put her science book?

  a on the shelf in her room

  b on the desk in her room

3 What did Jack think of the science test?

  a that it was easy and he did OK

  b that it was difficult but he did OK

4 What did Sophie think of the movie?

  a She really liked it.

  b She thought that it was boring.

5 Did Oscar go to the Science Museum?

  a Yes, he did.

  b No, he didn't.

6 Which project did Helen do last week?

  a science

  b math

1 Work with a friend. Read the fact file. Then choose your questions and ask and answer.

ISAAC NEWTON (1643–1727)

Born: England

Jobs: scientist, mathematician, astronomer

Worked at: the University of Cambridge

Discovered:
- the laws of gravity
- that light is made up of different colors

Described: the three laws of motion

Died: England

STUDENT A

- When and where was Isaac Newton born?
- Where did he work?
- What did he discover?

STUDENT B

- What jobs did Isaac Newton have?
- What did he describe?
- When and where did he die?

2 Read about Mary Anning. Choose one of her <u>underlined</u> discoveries and draw a picture of it. Use your imagination!

Mary Anning: *The World's Greatest Fossil Hunter*

Mary was born in England in 1799. When she was a child, Mary looked for fossils on the beach with her dad and brother. They collected them and then sold them. When Mary was twelve, she uncovered a long skeleton. It belonged to an ancient creature. Scientists named it <u>ichthyosaur, meaning "fish lizard."</u> As an adult, Mary discovered fossils of many more creatures, for example, the <u>pterodactyl (a flying reptile)</u> and the <u>plesiosaur (a sea creature with a very long neck)</u>. Mary died in England in 1847.

3 Work with a friend. Talk about your picture.

What did you draw?

I drew a pterodactyl – a flying reptile.

Why did you choose a pterodactyl?

I liked the idea that it flew.

Use the **past progressive** to talk about events that were happening at a particular moment in the past. Form the past progressive with **was** / **were** + **verb** + **ing**.

*I / he / she **was watching** a movie about Pompeii.*

*We / you / they **were watching** a play in the theater.*

Yes/No questions are formed with **was** / **were** + **verb** + **ing**.

***Were** you **feeling** all right yesterday afternoon? Yes, I was. / No, I wasn't.*

Form "Wh" questions by putting **where**, **what**, **why**, etc., before **was** / **were** + **verb** + **ing**.

***What were** you **doing** yesterday at two o'clock?*

1 Circle the correct verb forms.

It was Monday morning, and we were **(1)** *(listening)* / *listened* to a story in our ancient history class. "And then," said Ms. Kremer, who **(2)** *were* / *was* standing in front of the long window, "Vesuvius erupted, and the people of the beautiful city of ...." She stopped and turned her head. "Ms. Kremer," said Martyn, "is that the fire alarm?" It was. We left our bags in the room and followed our teacher to the emergency exit. Smoke was **(3)** *came* / *coming* up the hallway. Outside, we could see what **(4)** *was* / *were* happening. The auditorium was on fire! Teachers **(5)** *were* / *was* running around. The firefighters arrived really quickly and worked hard. They couldn't save the auditorium, but the most important thing was that everyone was safe. For the next few days, it was all we could talk about. "What were you doing when you **(6)** *heard* / *hearing* the alarm?" we asked, excited to tell our stories again, all thoughts of Vesuvius and the people of Pompeii forgotten.

2 Complete the sentences with a verb from the box in the past progressive form.

> listen ~~sit~~ do rise shout tell

Judith Tom said there was a fire at your school. What happened?

Daniella Yes, it was incredible! We **(1)** _____ were sitting _____ in Ms. Kremer's class …

Judith What **(2)** _____ you _____?

Daniella We **(3)** _____ to the story of Vesuvius. Ms. Kremer

(4) _____ us about the famous volcano when the fire alarm went off!

Judith What happened next?

Daniella We went outside with all the other students and stood in our groups. All the teachers were there. They **(5)** _____, "Move away from the building quickly! Move away, please!" The smoke **(6)** _____ above the auditorium.

3 Correct the sentences.

1 My parents were drove when they saw the accident.

    My parents were driving when they saw the accident._____

2 When the storm came, I am walking through the park.

   _____

3 What was you doing last night at six o'clock?

   _____

4 When the lights went out, I were doing my homework.

   _____

5 I was watch a movie when the fire started.

   _____

6 We was having dinner when we heard the news.

   _____

4 Answer the questions.

1 What were you doing at 9 o'clock this morning? _____

2 What were you doing yesterday morning at 10 o'clock? _____

3 What were you doing two days ago at 4 p.m.? _____

4 What were you doing a week ago at 7 o'clock in the evening? _____

5 What were you doing four days ago at lunchtime? _____

Two Simultaneous Actions with *While*

While I was reading a book, Jack was listening to music.

Language Focus

Words such as **and** and **but** are **conjunctions**. They connect words, phrases, and parts of a sentence. **While** is a conjunction. Use it to talk about two actions happening simultaneously (which means "at the same time").

While I was chatting with my friend, my dog was running after a ball.

1 Correct the sentences.

1 While I were doing my homework, my brothers were watching a movie.

   While I was doing my homework, my brothers were watching a movie.

2 While my father was writing an email, my sister is talking on the phone.

   _____

3 While I play a computer game, my mother was making a cup of tea.

   _____

4 While was Jane swimming, we were playing volleyball on the beach.

   _____

5 While I am studying for my science test, my friends were at the movies.

   _____

6 While Marco and Otto are watching the soccer game, I was reading a book.

   _____

2 Complete the sentences with a verb from the box in the past progressive form.

> talk   drink   cut   play   ~~read~~   sleep

1 While I _____ **was reading** _____ about volcanoes, Mom was painting.
2 While Mom was doing that, our cat _____ soundly under a tree.
3 While the cat was doing that, my brother and sister _____ soccer.
4 While my brother and sister were doing that, Grandma _____ a cup of coffee.
5 While Grandma was doing that, Grandpa _____ to Uncle Caspar.
6 While Grandpa was doing that, Dad _____ the grass.

3 Make sentences using the information in the table.

While	I my friends my teacher my sister my mom and dad my cousin	watch a movie play basketball send a text message play computer games sit in the yard eat a sandwich	my brother my grandma I my friend my dog my grandpa	sleep read a book wash the dishes drink a glass of water play the guitar run in the yard

1 While I was playing basketball, my dog was running in the yard.
2 _____
3 _____
4 _____
5 _____
6 _____

4 Write sentences with *while* using the following verbs: *play, watch, do, eat, study, read.*

1 While I was reading about a flood, my friend was reading about an avalanche.
2 _____
3 _____
4 _____
5 _____
6 _____

Reading: A Story

1 Read the story. Answer the questions.

The Day the
MOUNTAIN EXPLODED

It began as a beautiful day. The sun was shining, and the sky was blue. Everything was quiet and peaceful in the old town where Katerina lived with her family. Their town was popular with visitors, who came to see its temples and theaters, its columns and fountains, all of which were almost 2,000 years old. Tourists also enjoyed the sight of the horses and carts, which were still used in the center of the town.

Katerina came from a family of merchants who sold fruit and vegetables in the market in the main square. The house the family lived in was small for eight people, but it was clean, and its windows, which faced the street, were always filled with vases of beautiful flowers. It was a simple life but a good one.

The people of the town couldn't remember the last eruption. The volcano, which rose above the town to the east, was not something that most people thought about. However, in the days before the disaster, one old man was thinking about it. "It's going to explode," said Constantine, who spent his days sitting on the steps of the theater in the main square. While the people of the town were buying food, he was pointing to the top of the volcano, from which smoke was rising. "Look," he said. "It's going to explode." The people were too busy with their lives to pay attention to what Constantine was saying. When the volcano erupted two days later, ash and lava covered everything and everyone in the town—everyone, that is, except for Katerina and her family, the only people who listened to Constantine's warning. While the ash was falling on the town, they were watching from a town in the mountains many, many miles away, sad to see what was happening but glad to be safe.

1 How old were the temples and theaters in the town? _____ almost 2,000 years old _____

2 What did Katerina's family sell? _____

3 Where did Katerina's family sell their produce? _____

4 How many people were there in Katerina's family? _____

5 Who warned the people about the volcano? _____

6 Who listened to the warning about the volcano? _____

1 Order the words to make expressions used to describe shock and surprise.

1 it / can't / believe / I / .   I can't believe it.

2 is / unbelievable / this / .   _____

3 really / is / happening / this / ?   _____

4 so / it's / awful / .   _____

5 a / it's / tragedy / .   _____

6 for / words / I'm / lost / .   _____

Help with Writing

When you write a story, think about how you order the information. For example, at the beginning of paragraph 3, we read, "The people of the town couldn't remember the last eruption." It is only in the next sentence that we read the word "volcano." Organizing sentences in this way makes the information more surprising for the reader.

2 Imagine you are Katerina. Write about leaving the town and watching the volcano erupt. Include expressions of surprise and the following information:

- what you took with you (e.g., food, clothes, books)
- what you thought when you were watching the volcano erupt
- what Constantine and people in your family said

_____

_____

_____

_____

_____

_____

_____

_____

_____

_____

_____

_____

_____

_____

Listening: Natural Disasters

1 🎧 **03** **Listen to Leo's story about his grandpa. Are sentences 1–6 true or false?**

1 Leo's grandpa was working in the United States. `t`

2 Leo's grandpa was thirty years old in 1980. ☐

3 He was interested in a volcano called
Mount St. Helens. ☐

4 Before the volcano erupted, there were
many earthquakes. ☐

5 When the volcano erupted, Leo's grandpa
was walking to his car. ☐

6 He took lots of photos of the volcano eruption. ☐

2 🎧 **04** **Listen to Sara's story. Complete the sentences with one word.**

1 Sara's town has a new _____*museum*_____.

2 Sara was there on the weekend. She was with her _____.

3 There were Greek and Roman _____. They were 2,000 years old.

4 Sara liked some _____ from an ancient Greek temple.

5 Sara was taking a photo of a Greek _____ when the earthquake started.

6 People covered their heads with their arms because _____ were falling to the floor.

1 **Look at the photos. Play the guessing game.**

> I was at home. I was reading my book. It was raining heavily outside. Suddenly, water came into the kitchen!

> There was a flood!

earthquake

volcano eruption

tornado

tsunami

flood

fire

2 **Choose a natural disaster from Activity 1. Imagine it happened in your town. Write answers. Then practice.**

1 When was it? _____

2 Where were you? _____

3 What were you doing? _____

4 Who was with you? _____

5 What happened? _____

6 What did you do? _____

3 **Work with a friend. Tell your stories. Use your answers from Activity 2.**

Help with Speaking

When you tell a story, you don't need to talk about everything that happened. Talk about the most important things, and let your friend listen to you. Give your friend time to imagine the events in your story.

> It was a Saturday morning. I was in the backyard. I was playing soccer with my brother. Suddenly, we smelled smoke. We looked up and saw that the smoke was coming from the volcano ...

2 Numbers 100–5,000,000

Language Focus

The **number system** is organized in tens:

1 10 100 1,000 10,000

Each number in the list above is ten times larger than the previous one.

When we write numerals, we use commas when there are four or more digits. For example, there is no comma in 300, but there is a comma in 3,000. To find the place to put the comma, count three spaces to the left from the end of the number. Place commas after every three digits:

3,000 30,000 3,000,000

When we write numbers as words, we do not use commas with round numbers.

40,000: forty thousand not ~~*forty, thousand*~~

When we write numbers as words, we add a hyphen to compound numbers between 21 and 99.

442: four hundred and forty-two 6,363: six thousand, three hundred and sixty-three

---

1   **Add the missing numbers to the sequences.**

1 500	5,000	50,000		**500,000**
2 1,000	10,000	_____	1,000,000
3 2,000	20,000	200,000	_____
4 300	3,000	30,000	_____
5 6	60	_____	6,000
6 80	800	8,000	_____

2 Match the numbers with the words.

1 300
2 2,500
3 11,350
4 78,328
5 386,422
6 4,500,000

a three hundred and eighty-six thousand, four hundred and twenty-two
b seventy-eight thousand, three hundred and twenty-eight
c two thousand, five hundred
d three hundred
e four million, five hundred thousand
f eleven thousand, three hundred and fifty

3 Write the numbers.

1 one hundred and eighty-two   182
2 four thousand, six hundred and seventy   _____
3 seventy-five thousand   _____
4 one hundred and ten thousand, eight hundred and forty   _____
5 three hundred and ten thousand, four hundred and forty-two _____
6 eight hundred and twenty thousand, one hundred and three   _____
7 two million   _____
8 four million, nine hundred and eighty-nine thousand,
    nine hundred and ninety-nine   _____

4 Write the words.

The Numbers Quiz

1 There are about 800,000 __eight hundred thousand__ people living in Guyana in South America.

2 Around 2,000,000 _____ people live in Manaus, the biggest city in the state of Amazonas.

3 Giant anteaters eat about 35,000 _____ ants and termites every day.

4 There are about 15,000 _____ jaguars left in the wild.

5 Around 150 _____ different ethnic groups live in the Congo Basin in Central Africa.

6 The Amazon River is about 6,400 _____ km long.

Have to / Had to Review

It's going to be hot. We **have to** take T-shirts, hats, sunglasses, and sunblock.

Language Focus

Use **have to** / **had to** to talk about something that somebody else tells you to do.

We **had to** take lots of water with us on the trip. Mr. Mathews said it was very important.

Do I / you / we / they **have to** go?   Yes, I / you / we / they do.

No, I / you / we / they don't.

Does he / she **have to** do it?   Yes, he / she does.

No, he / she doesn't.

1 Match the questions with the answers.

1 Do you have to help your parents at home?

2 Do you have to do homework every night?

3 Does your brother have to clean his room?

4 Do you have to go shopping with your parents?

5 Do you have to wear a uniform to school?

6 Does your sister have to make her bed?

a No, I don't. They usually go with my older brother and sister.

b Yes, she does. My parents always say, "Your room is messy. Please clean it up."

c No, he doesn't. My parents don't mind if our rooms are messy.

d Yes, I do. I have to do the dishes and clean my room.

e We had to wear one last year, but it's different now.

f I usually have to do some studying Monday to Friday but not on the weekend.

2 Correct the sentences.

1 Last week, I have to study hard.

   Last week, I had to study hard.

2 Do you has to clean your room?

   _____

3 My parents have get up very early every morning.

   _____

4 My sister have to take the dog for a walk before school.

   _____

5 Last night, I had to wrote a story for my English class.

   _____

6 My brothers doesn't have to help in the kitchen. They have to clean the bathroom.

   _____

7 Yesterday, I had clean my room. It took a long time!

   _____

8 I have to help cook dinner, but I haven't to do the dishes.

   _____

9 We don't has to get up early tomorrow. It's Saturday.

   _____

10 Do your parents have to working on the weekend?

   _____

3 What do you have to do at home? Write four sentences.

   1 _____

   2 _____

   3 _____

   4 _____

4 What did you have to do at school last week? Write four sentences.

   1 _____

   2 _____

   3 _____

   4 _____

Reading: A Tourism Advertisement

1 Read the advertisement. Write *t* (true) or *f* (false). Correct the false sentences.

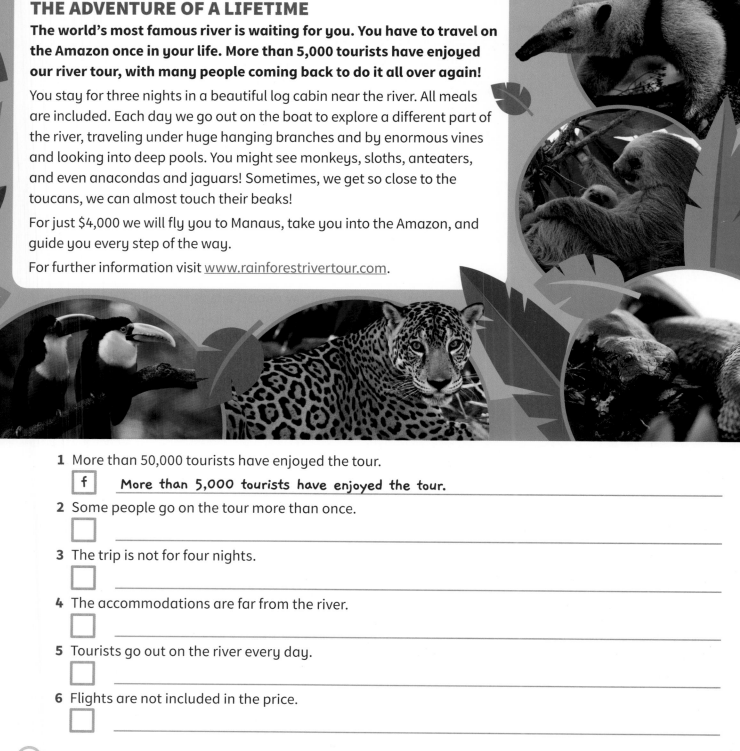

THE AMAZON RAINFOREST RIVER TOUR!

THE ADVENTURE OF A LIFETIME

The world's most famous river is waiting for you. You have to travel on the Amazon once in your life. More than 5,000 tourists have enjoyed our river tour, with many people coming back to do it all over again!

You stay for three nights in a beautiful log cabin near the river. All meals are included. Each day we go out on the boat to explore a different part of the river, traveling under huge hanging branches and by enormous vines and looking into deep pools. You might see monkeys, sloths, anteaters, and even anacondas and jaguars! Sometimes, we get so close to the toucans, we can almost touch their beaks!

For just $4,000 we will fly you to Manaus, take you into the Amazon, and guide you every step of the way.

For further information visit www.rainforestrivertour.com.

1 More than 50,000 tourists have enjoyed the tour.

[f]   More than 5,000 tourists have enjoyed the tour.

2 Some people go on the tour more than once.

[ ]

3 The trip is not for four nights.

[ ]

4 The accommodations are far from the river.

[ ]

5 Tourists go out on the river every day.

[ ]

6 Flights are not included in the price.

[ ]

1 Order the words to make phrases used in advertisements for vacations.

1 on / tour / wonderful / come / our / . Come on our wonderful tour.

2 for / waiting / are / what / you / ? _____

3 up / today / sign / . _____

4 vacation / the / of / lifetime / a / it's / . _____

5 of / thousands / customers / satisfied / . _____

Help with Writing

Advertisements often use the language of obligation as a way of making people want to do something. Notice how the advertisement for the Amazon Rainforest River Tour uses the sentence "You have to travel on the Amazon once in your life."

2 Write an advertisement for a tour of a place in your country where people can see different animals. Use the advertisement for the Amazon Rainforest River Tour to help you. Include the following information:

- where the place is
- what is special or interesting about it
- what activities you can do there
- which animals you can see there
- the cost of the trip

_____
_____
_____
_____
_____
_____
_____
_____
_____
_____
_____
_____
_____
_____
_____
_____

Listening: Jungle Adventure

1 🎧 05 Listen to the conversation. Circle the correct words.

DID YOU KNOW ... ?

1 The Amazon rainforest gets between 150 / (1,500) and 3,000 millimeters of rain every year.

2 A bristlecone pine in California is more than 500 / 4,800 years old!

3 A green anaconda can weigh more than 200 / 300 kilograms.

4 There are about 400,000 / 40,000 kinds of beetles in the world.

5 Spider monkeys live in the Amazon rainforest and have long tails. Their tails can be up to 90 / 190 centimeters long!

6 There are about 12,000 / 10,000 kinds of ants on our planet.

rain in the Amazon

bristlecone pine

green anaconda

beetle

spider monkey

ants

2 🎧 06 What does Alex have to do before his trip? Listen and check ✓ or put an ✗.

I have to ...	
pack my things	✓
take a shower and get dressed	☐
make breakfast	☐
take my boots	☐
pack the car	☐
wash and dry the dishes	☐
clean my room	☐

1 Work with a friend. Imagine you are going to the Amazon rainforest. Check ☑ what you have to take with you. Then say why.

boots ☑

a soccer ball ☐

food and water ☐

shirts with long sleeves ☐

a hat ☐

mosquito repellent ☐

computer games ☐

sunblock ☐

a backpack ☐

a kite ☐

> We have to take boots with us.

> Why?

> Because there are dangerous snakes around!

2 With your friend, think of four more things to add to the list in Activity 1.

> Let's take a camera with us.

> Good idea! We can take some nice photos.

3 With your friend, choose five things you would like to do on your trip to the Amazon. Use the ideas below and your ideas.

> I'd like to swim in the river. What about you?

> I don't want to do that. We have to be careful. There are anacondas in the river!

see jaguars

look for tarantulas

see toucans

see anacondas

go on a boat on the river

meet people who live in the rainforest

swim in the river

take hundreds of photos

3 Going to Review

Are you **going to go** to the festival on Saturday?

Language Focus

Use **going to** + **infinitive** for plans and predictions.

*Who is **going to win** the soccer championship?*

Plans

*I'm **going to study** hard all weekend. I have tests next week.*

*We're **going to plan** a surprise party for Dad's birthday.*

Predictions

*It's **going to rain**. Look at those clouds!*

*I didn't sleep very well last night. I'm **going to be** tired today.*

1 **Complete the blog post with the verbs from the box.**

see ~~be~~ have play come visit

HOME	ABOUT	BLOG	GALLERY	CONTACT	🔍

This weekend is going to (1) _____ **be** _____ amazing. We have so many plans!
On Friday, Osman, Noelia, and I are going to a concert. Who are we going to
(2) _____? Yes, that's right! The Marvins! My favorite band. Tom can't
come because he's going to (3) _____ his cousins, but he and I are going
to (4) _____ in a doubles tennis tournament on Saturday. Mom and Dad
are going to (5) _____ and watch us play. They're very excited.
On Sunday, we're going to (6) _____ dinner in a new restaurant by
the river. It's to celebrate my sister's twelfth birthday! What a weekend!

2 Write the following sentences in the negative form.

1 We're going to play basketball. <u>**We're not going to play basketball.**</u>

2 I'm going to buy a new guitar. _____

3 My brother's going to study math in college. _____

4 My mom's going to start her new job soon. _____

5 My friends and I are going to watch the championship game. _____

_____

6 My dad's going to make a cake with my sister. _____

7 My cousins are going to spend a week in Buenos Aires. _____

_____

8 We're going to visit my grandparents in Istanbul. _____

9 I'm going to study Arabic next year. _____

10 My sister's going to start her driving lessons tomorrow. _____

_____

3 Order the questions.

1 going / do / your / friend / weekend / to / what / on / is / best / the / ?

<u>**What is your best friend going to do on the weekend?**</u>

2 tonight / you / what / going / do / to / are / ?

_____

3 you / vacation / to / where / for / your / go / summer / going / are / ?

_____

4 next / languages / in / school / you / what / are / study / to / going / year / ?

_____

5 this / weekend / the / you / going / friends / to / which / meet / are / ?

_____

6 family / special / when / going / is / meal / your / have / to / a / ?

_____

4 Answer the questions from Activity 3.

1 _____

2 _____

3 _____

4 _____

5 _____

6 _____

Time: *Past* and *To* the Hour

What time is it, Jonny?

It's ten to eleven.

Language Focus

Use **past** and **to** to talk about the time.

*It's ten **past** five* (meaning "It's ten minutes past the hour of five o'clock, or 5:10").

*It's twenty **to** seven* (meaning "It's twenty minutes before the hour of seven o'clock, or 6:40").

In informal spoken English, it is common to use abbreviated forms like "It's ten past" or "It's twenty to," if the people you are talking to have a general idea of what time it is.

1 Write the times using *past* and *to*.

1 10:50 _It's ten to eleven._

2 9:05 _____

3 7:40 _____

4 12:10 _____

5 4:50 _____

6 3:20 _____

2 Correct the times.

1 6:40   It's twenty past six.   _It's twenty to seven._
2 8:10   It's five past eight.   _____
3 3:05   It's five to three.   _____
4 1:20   It's twenty to one.   _____
5 2:50   It's five to three.   _____
6 8:20   It's ten past eight.   _____

3 Write the underlined times in words.

Malcolm had a problem with time. "Oh, no!" he would say when he woke up. "It's **(1) 7:20**! I'm going to be late for school!" "It's **(2) 8:10**, Malcolm!" his teacher would say. "Why can't you get here on time?"

Malcolm was late for everything. He missed the great new science-fiction movie because he got to the movie theater at **(3) 6:40**, forty minutes late! He was late for the final game of the soccer season. "Malcolm," the coach said, "it's **(4) 3:20**! The game started twenty minutes ago!" "Sorry," said Malcolm. He said "sorry" a lot. He said "sorry" to Dr. Morgan, the dentist. "Your appointment was for **(5) 4:50**, Malcolm, not **(6) 5:10**."

He said "sorry" to Dr. Nadal, the doctor. "Your appointment was for **(7) 12:40**, Malcolm, not **(8) 1:05**."

Malcolm loved birthday parties and decided to organize one in his favorite café to celebrate his thirteenth birthday. "Come at **(9) 7:20**," he told all his friends. "OK, Malcolm," his friends said. "We'll be there!" But no one arrived. Malcolm waited in the café. Ten minutes, twenty minutes, thirty minutes ... Where was everyone? "Surprise!" said his friends when they finally arrived. "But it's **(10) 8:05**!" said Malcolm. "You're forty-five minutes late!" "Now you know how it feels," said his friend Jenny, smiling. Malcolm was never late again.

1 _twenty past seven_   5 _____   9 _____
2 _____   6 _____   10 _____
3 _____   7 _____
4 _____   8 _____

4 Answer the questions.

1 What time do you get up on weekdays? _____
2 What time do you start school? _____
3 What time do you come home from school? _____
4 What time do you do your homework? _____
5 What time do you get up on the weekend? _____
6 What time do you go to bed? _____

Reading: An Email

1 Read the email. Complete the fact file.

chen@chinamail.com

The Marvins Concert!

Hi, Chen,

How are you? I hope the Spanish test went well. I have a question: what are you doing on Friday? Osman, Karl, and I are going to see The Marvins. Do you know them? They're a great rock band. You can watch some of their videos online.

Would you like to come to the concert with us? We're going to meet at the bus station at twenty to six. It takes half an hour to get to the theater. The show is going to start at ten past seven. It will be great, Chen.

The Marvins have a lot of fans, and they are a lot of fun. It will be really busy on stage. The band has six backup singers as well as three dancers! Marvin will be in the spotlight; he's the lead singer. Jay plays the electric guitar, Kelly plays the bass guitar, and the drummer is named Sal. Her drum kit is bright orange. I love it! Osman says he wants to work for the band as a bodyguard in the future!

Let me know if you'd like to come on Friday. I hope you are well.

Best wishes,

Noelia

Day of the Concert	Friday
Time of the Concert	
Meeting Where?	
Who Is Going?	
Members of the Band	

1 Match 1–5 with a–e to make phrases for accepting an invitation or expressing interest in an idea.

1 Thanks for

2 I'd love

3 That sounds

4 What a

5 It sounds like

a great idea.

b really exciting.

c inviting me.

d a great plan.

e to come.

Help with Writing

We often write emails very quickly. It is a good idea to proofread your emails before you send them. Proofreading is checking written material for errors.

2 Imagine you are Chen. You want to go to the concert. Write an email in response to Noelia's. Use one or more of the phrases from Activity 1 and ask Noelia for the following information:

- how much the tickets cost
- what time the concert is going to finish
- how you are going to get home
- the names of the band's best songs

Listening: Music

1 🎧 **07** **Listen to the interview. Answer the questions.**

1 When is Chris Frank going to start recording his new album?

next week

2 What is he going to call it?

_____

3 What music genre is the album going to be?

_____

4 What is Chris going to learn this year?

_____

5 When Chris isn't on tour, what time does he usually get up?

_____

6 When Chris isn't on tour, what time does he usually go to bed?

_____

2 🎧 **08** **Listen to the conversation. Complete the sentences.**

1 Jake and Daisy are going to a _____ concert _____ .

2 They are going to leave at _____ .

3 The concert is going to start at _____ .

4 They are going to have _____ before the show.

5 Daisy's cousin is a _____ _____ in the band.

6 Daisy isn't going to go on the _____ and dance.

1 Work with a friend. Choose one poster each. Make questions about your concert using the words in the box. Then ask and answer.

> who / see?   where?   time / start?
> time / finish?   how much / tickets?

> Who are you going to see?

> I'm going to see The Bodyguards.

STUDENT A

Come and see
THE BODYGUARDS
at the Old Soccer Stadium!

When: This Saturday
Start time: 6:20
Finish time: 7:20
Tickets: $10

STUDENT B

DON'T MISS
THE ROCKING CLOCKS
at the Spotlight Theater!

WHEN: This Sunday
START TIME: 12:15
FINISH TIME: 1:30
TICKETS: $13

2 Design a poster for a concert you want to see. Include the information on the left and your own ideas.

- name of the band
- place and day of the concert
- time the concert starts
- time the concert finishes
- price of the tickets

3 Show your poster to a friend. Talk about your plans.

> On Friday, I'm going to see Submarine Jazz. The musicians play underwater! The concert starts at quarter to six, and it finishes at half past seven. It's going to be at the Blue Sports Center, and the tickets are $15. What about you?

4 Ordinal Numbers

When is your birthday?

DECEMBER

It's December third.

Language Focus

Use **ordinal numbers** to talk about the position of something or someone in a series, such as dates or competitors in a race.

*My brother finished **second** in the 200 meters at the swim competition.*

When is your birthday?   *It's on June **fourth**.*

Numbers used for a quantity of something are called **cardinal numbers**.

Cardinal Number	Ordinal Number	Cardinal Number	Ordinal Number
1	*first*	4	*fourth*
2	*second*	5	*fifth*
3	*third*	6	*sixth*

In general, ordinal numbers are formed by adding **th** to the cardinal number: **ten – tenth**.

First, **second**, and **third** are exceptions and do not follow the **th** rule.

The ordinal for eight is **eighth**, not **eightth**.

The ordinal for nine is **ninth**, not **nineth**.

The ordinal for twelve is **twelfth**, not **twelveth**.

In a compound cardinal, use a hyphen, e.g., **thirty-third**.

If a cardinal number ends in **y**, change the **y** to an **i** and then add **eth**.

twenty   **twentieth**   *thirty*   **thirtieth**   *forty*   **fortieth**

---

1   Write the ordinal numbers.

1 7   _____seventh_____   **3** 22 _____   **5** 38 _____

2 15 _____   **4** 31 _____   **6** 44 _____

2 Write the dates with ordinal numbers.

1 January 3 — _January third_

2 May 5 — _____

3 July 29 — _____

4 February 23 — _____

5 November 8 — _____

6 August 30 — _____

3 Replace the underlined phrases with dates written in full.

Hi, Grandma,

I have so much to tell you! On **(1)** March 2, Florence won her race at the swim competition. She was amazing! **(2)** The next day, my soccer team got to the final of the Morley Cup. The game will be on **(3)** May 4. I can't wait. On **(4)** the day after the final, I'm going on a field trip to Amsterdam.

Don't forget all the birthdays coming up, Grandma! It's Florence's on **(5)** April 25. Mine is **(6)** three days later!

Love, Sophia

1 — _March second_

2 — _____

3 — _____

4 — _____

5 — _____

6 — _____

4 Complete your calendar. Write one activity for each day.

MAY

7 Monday	
8 Tuesday	
9 Wednesday	
10 Thursday	
11 Friday	
12 Saturday	
13 Sunday	

5 Answer the questions.

1 What are you doing on May eighth? _____

2 What are you doing on May tenth? _____

3 What are you doing on May twelfth? _____

4 What are you doing on May thirteenth? _____

Zero Conditional

> **If you mix** the blue liquid with the red liquid, something incredible happens.

Language Focus

Use the **zero conditional** to talk about things that are always true. The zero conditional tells us that if one thing happens, another thing always happens as a result.

This is the form of the sentence: **if** + **simple present** + **simple present**:

If you mix red and blue, *you get* purple.

---

1 **Correct the sentences.**

1 If Mom can't go for a run in the morning, she feel unhappy.

   If Mom can't go for a run in the morning, she feels unhappy.

2 If my brother enjoying a movie, he talks about it for hours.

   _____

3 If you doesn't exercise, you put on weight.

   _____

4 If you standing in the rain, you get wet.

   _____

5 If Sam ran in the summer, he gets very hot.

   _____

6 If I travel in a car, I felt sick.

   _____

2 Choose the correct option to complete the sentences.

1 If babies are hungry,
   a they are crying.
   (b) they cry.
   c they cried.

2 If you mix hydrogen and oxygen,
   a you get water.
   b you got water.
   c you're getting water.

3 If students are late for class,
   a Mr. Marks gets angry.
   b Mr. Marks get angry.
   c Mr. Marks got angry.

4 If plants don't get enough water,
   a it dies.
   b they died.
   c they die.

5 If we don't drink,
   a we've got thirsty.
   b we got thirsty.
   c we get thirsty.

3 Complete the text with the verbs from the box.

> do ~~go~~ think put need know feel ask

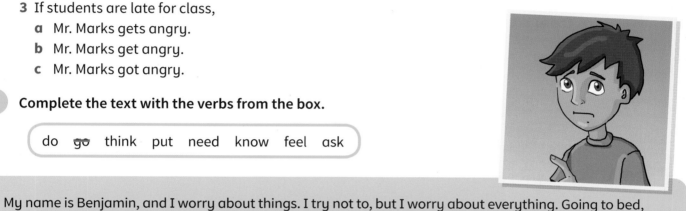

My name is Benjamin, and I worry about things. I try not to, but I worry about everything. Going to bed, for example. If I **(1)** _____go_____ to bed early, I can't go to sleep. If I go to bed late, I **(2)** _____ tired the next day. If I am in bed at exactly the right time, I **(3)** _____, "Is this exactly the right time?" I worry about my schoolwork, too. If I **(4)** _____ one hour of homework every night, I **(5)** _____ myself, "Was that enough?" If I do two hours of homework, I say, "Mom, I think I've done too much homework tonight." I never know what is the right thing to do because I am a worrier. "Oh, what a beautiful day," my friends say in the springtime when the weather gets warmer. "If it's really sunny," I say to myself, "I **(6)** _____ to put sunblock on, but if I **(7)** _____ sunblock on, I get it in my eyes." "Oh, Benjamin," my friends say. "Why do you worry about everything so much?" "I don't know," I say. "If I don't worry about things, I don't **(8)** _____ what else to do."

4 Complete the sentences.

1 If you exercise, **you feel better.** _____
2 If you read lots of good books, _____
3 If you catch a cold, _____
4 If you don't get enough sleep, _____
5 If you eat a balanced diet, _____
6 If you keep to a routine, _____
7 If you eat too much, _____
8 If you work too hard, _____

1 Read the invitation. Answer the questions.

You Are Invited to
JANA'S 12TH BIRTHDAY PARTY

If you're free, come and join us!

WHEN
Saturday, May 1, between 2 p.m. and 6 p.m.

WHERE
The Hong Kong Space Restaurant on Main Street, where the waiters are robots and nobody eats with a knife and fork!

WHAT WE'LL EAT
There'll be delicious Chinese food for everyone, practice eating with chopsticks, and special Chinese cookies to take home.
RSVP Samantha (Jana's mom) at sam@homemail.com.

1 How old will Jana be?   12
2 When is the party?
3 Where is the party?
4 What is the party for?
5 What is different about the restaurant?
6 If people want to go to the party, who can they contact?

1 Complete the table with information about you.

Date of Birthday	
Games You Like Playing at Parties	
Music You Like Listening to at Parties	
What You Enjoy Eating at Parties	
What You Enjoy Drinking at Parties	

Help with Writing

When we write invitations, we often include the abbreviation "RSVP" at the end, followed by a name and contact details. RSVP stands for the French expression "Répondez s'il vous plaît," which means "Please reply."

2 Imagine it is your birthday next week. Use the information in Activity 1 and the invitation to Jana's party to help you write an invitation to your birthday party.

Listening: Food in Space

1 🎧 **09** **Listen. Are sentences 1–6 true or false?**

1 Polly went into space in the summer.

2 Polly has been to space three times.

3 Polly's birthday is on the last day of July.

4 Some waiters at Cosmic are robots.

5 Polly went for a space walk on August 1st.

6 Polly had a pizza candy for lunch on August 2nd.

t
☐
☐
☐
☐
☐

2 🎧 **10** **Listen and write C (Cosmic) or S (Solar).**

1 This restaurant is in a hotel.   C

2 In this restaurant, people eat candy that tastes like real food. _____

3 If you are eating in this restaurant, you don't need a knife, a fork, or a spoon. _____

4 This restaurant is the newest in space. _____

5 You can't eat in this restaurant before May 3rd. _____

6 If you want to finish your dinner quickly, go to this restaurant. _____

7 If you want to enjoy a nice view, go to this restaurant. _____

8 If you reserve a table here before the end of April, you'll get something special. _____

1 Look at the photos. Play the guessing game. Use the words from the box and your ideas.

> a spoon   dessert
> a waiter/waitress   chopsticks
> a knife and a fork

> If you have this, you need a knife and a fork.

> Is it number 2, a steak?

> Yes, it is!

Chinese food

a steak

chicken soup

a restaurant

strawberries

crackers

2 Choose and check ☑ an appetizer, a main course, and a dessert from the Solar menu. Talk to a friend. Are any of your choices the same?

> What did you choose for your appetizer?

> I chose cracker soup. What about you?

Help with Speaking

When you speak, try to use the new words that you have learned. You remember words more easily when you use them!

3 Work with a friend. Order your meals from Activity 2.

> Hello. What would you like for your appetizer?

> I'd like the cracker soup, please.

> Of course. And for your main course?

> Can I have the chocolate pizza, please?

OUR SOLAR MENU

SOLAR Appetizers
- [ ] cracker soup
- [ ] strawberry soup

SOLAR Main Courses
- [ ] chocolate pizza
- [ ] lemonade salad

SOLAR Desserts
- [ ] cheese ice cream
- [ ] egg cake

5 Be made of ... / Be used for ...

What's that made of, Mom?

Wool. I really like it!

Language Focus

Use **made of** and **used for** when describing different aspects of an object.
When talking about the material used to manufacture the object, use **made of**.

*These pants are **made of** cotton.*

When talking about the function of an object, use **used for**.

*Scarves are **used for** keeping your neck warm in cold weather.*

Use **made of** with various materials: ***made of** wool / plastic / glass / cotton.*

Use **used for** + **verb** + **ing**: ***used for** keeping things in / keeping food cold.*

---

1 Complete the sentences with the words and phrases from the box.

> making music   ~~leather~~   protecting your eyes   glass
> cutting things   plastic   metal   opening and closing doors

1 Shoes are made of <u>leather</u>   .
2 Guitars are used for _____ .
3 Sunglasses are used for _____ .
4 Knives are made of _____ .
5 Supermarket bags are made of _____ .
6 Keys are used for _____ .
7 Windows are made of wood and _____ .
8 Scissors are used for _____ .

2 Match the objects with the descriptions.

1 This is made of plastic and metal. It's used for making a kind of hot drink.   e ___

2 This is made of leather and metal. It's used for keeping your pants up.   ___

3 This is made of metal and cloth. It's used for keeping you dry in wet weather.   ___

4 This is made of metal and glass. It's used for looking at your reflection.   ___

5 These are made of wool or cotton. They are used for keeping your feet warm.   ___

6 This is made of wood and glass. It's used for storing things such as cups and bowls.   ___

3 Correct the sentences.

1 Pens is made of plastic.

   Pens are made of plastic.

2 Vases are use for putting flowers in.

   _____

3 Knit caps are using for keeping your head warm in winter.

   _____

4 Saddles are make of leather.

   _____

5 Pencils made of wood.

   _____

6 Tables are used putting things on.

   _____

7 T-shirts are often makes of cotton.

   _____

8 Flash drives are used of storing data.

   _____

4 Complete each sentence with a suitable word.

1 Chairs are made of _____ .

2 Bags are used for _____ .

3 Spoons are used for _____ .

4 Shirts are made of _____ .

5 Gloves are made of _____ .

6 Pencils are used for _____ .

Possessive Apostrophes

The boy's boots are made of real leather.

Language Focus

Use **possessive apostrophes** to talk about things that belong to a particular person. *Is this Mom's hat?*

If a noun is plural, the apostrophe goes after the **s**.

the girls' badges (meaning the badges of more than one girl)

If referring to someone whose name ends in **s**, you can either add an apostrophe after the **s** or add an apostrophe and another **s**.

James' car or *James's car*

1 Put the words in the correct order to make sentences.

1 full / Esra's / of / books / is / house / .

　Esra's house is full of books.

2 brother / know / do / Jon's / you / ?

_____

3 new / bike / Mom's / like / I / really / .

_____

4 hat / Alex's / is / where / ?

_____

5 is / broken / racket / Javi's / tennis / .

_____

6 of / gold / made / is / Tom's / badge / .

_____

7 named / Sheriff / is / Ana's / cat / .

_____

8 the / closet / in / is / Hasan's / jacket / .

_____

2 Add possessive apostrophes.

1 Kates smartphone was very expensive.

Kate's smartphone was very expensive.

2 Carlas brothers are much older than her.

_____

3 Michaels dog is very friendly.

_____

4 My grandparents house is very small.

_____

5 My parents car needs to be repaired.

_____

6 Williams piano is very old, but he loves it.

_____

7 My sisters bedrooms are on the second floor of the house.

_____

8 Moms computer is better than mine.

_____

3 Read the information and choose the correct sentence.

1 Sam says, "I have two brothers. They are very tall."
   (a) The boy's brothers are tall.   b The boys' brothers are tall.

2 Martina says, "I have two sisters. One of them has a red scarf."
   a The girl's sister has a red scarf.   b The girl's sisters have red scarves.

3 Lola says, "My friends all have new phones."
   a The girl's friends have new phones.   b The girl's friend has a new phone.

4 Mark and Jack say, "Our history teacher wears big glasses."
   a The boy's teacher wears big glasses.   b The boys' teacher wears big glasses.

5 Alana says, "My dogs like playing with the ball."
   a The girl's dogs like playing with the ball. b The girls' dog likes playing with the ball.

6 Alice and Cathy say, "Our town is a nice place."
   a The girl's town is a nice place.   b The girls' town is a nice place.

4 Write sentences about your friends and family using the possessive apostrophe.

1 _____

2 _____

3 _____

4 _____

1 Read the classified advertisements. Match the objects with the information.

FOR SALE

PAIR OF BOOTS. Made of fake leather! In very good condition. Beautiful design. Only been worn a few times.
$25. Tel: 642-3321.

ACOUSTIC GUITAR. Made of rosewood. Only been played at home. Not been used for playing in concerts. In excellent condition.
$250. Tel: 771-1624.

SHERIFF'S COSTUME. Perfect for costume parties! Set includes toy pistol, badge, handcuffs, and a sheriff's hat.
$50. Great price! Tel: 502-7892.

ELECTRIC GUITAR. Incredible instrument, made of glass! Only one ever made. Never been played.
$1,000. Tel: 444-1098.

BEAUTIFUL WOODEN WAGON. Made of mahogany. Carved by hand. Ten centimeters in height. In perfect condition.
$80. Tel: 887 521.

SADDLE. Made of the finest leather. Has been used, but still in good condition.
$30. Tel: 887-4425.

1	pair of boots	f	a the smallest object
2	acoustic guitar	___	b a set of several objects
3	sheriff's costume	___	c not been used out of the house
4	electric guitar	___	d the most expensive object
5	wagon	___	e made of leather
6	saddle	___	f the cheapest object

1 Rewrite 1–6 so that they are similar to phrases used in classified advertisements.

1 It's made of wood. _____Made of wood._____

2 It's in perfect condition. _____

3 A bike and a helmet. _____

4 Piano. It has not been used much. _____

5 A beautiful scarf. It's made of wool. _____

6 Telephone: 443-1725. _____

Help with Writing

We write classified advertisements by using a special abbreviated style. This means that we include only the most important information. We usually leave out the verb **be**, auxiliary verbs such as **have**, and the articles **a / an** and **the**.

2 Write a classified advertisement for some items you would like to sell. Use the examples on the Reading page to help you. Include the following information:

- what each item is
- what each item is made of
- how much each item costs
- a telephone number

Listening: Sheriffs and Robbers

1 🎧 11 **Listen and write the colors.**

What Did They Wear?	Big John Warren	Bison Bill
1	brown	black
2		
3		
4		
5		

2 🎧 12 **Listen to the story. Circle the correct answers.**

1 What were Bella Three-Trees' boots made of?

  a brown leather   **(b)** black leather

2 What did Bella use the bottle for?

  a holding cold tea   **b** holding cold coffee

3 Which word describes the robbers' horses?

  a fast   **b** slow

4 What did Bella use her rope for?

  a tying her horse   **b** stealing things

5 What did Bella steal?

  a only things made of glass   **b** some things made of glass and other things made of metal

6 Who was Gray Shelly?

  a the sheriff's horse   **b** Bella's horse

1 **Play the description game. Use the words below the pictures.**

Sheriff Brown.

Sheriff Brown's bottle is made of glass. It's used for holding water.

Sheriff Brown	**Sheriff Holliday**	**Sheriff Drew**	**Sheriff Brady**
bottle	badge	rope	holster
saddle	wagon	barrel	handcuffs

2 **Draw a picture of a sheriff. Talk about your picture.**

This is Sheriff Henry Adams. Henry's badge is made of silver, and his boots are made of leather. He's wearing …

3 **Show your picture to a friend. Ask and answer.**

What is the sheriff holding?

He's holding a pair of metal handcuffs.

What are they used for?

They're used for taking robbers to jail.

6 Should / Shouldn't

You should take an umbrella, Poppy. I think it's going to rain later.

Language Focus

Use **should** / **shouldn't** to give someone advice, make suggestions, or talk about the right thing to do in a particular situation.

*You **should** drink more water on hot days.*

Should and **shouldn't** are followed by the **infinitive without to**.

*You **should study** really hard for the Spanish test,* not ~~You should to study really hard for the Spanish test.~~

1 **Complete the sentences with *should* or *shouldn't*.**

1 You _____shouldn't_____ be rude to your sister.

2 You _____ go out without a coat and scarf. It's really cold today.

3 You have a big day of tests tomorrow. You _____ go to bed early and get a good night's sleep.

4 If your foot hurts, you _____ play soccer this afternoon.

5 It's really sunny today. You _____ put some sunblock on.

6 If you go to Turkey, you _____ visit Izmir. It's a beautiful place.

7 You _____ exercise a few times a week.

8 You _____ eat too many chocolates. You'll feel sick.

2 Circle the correct verb.

To learn a **language well**, ...

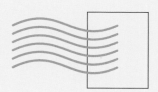

1. you *should / shouldn't* let it become boring. Enjoy yourself!

2. you *should / shouldn't* be afraid to make mistakes.

3. you *should / shouldn't* watch movies and listen to songs in the language.

4. you *should / shouldn't* read a lot.

5. you *should / shouldn't* take every opportunity to speak to people.

6. you *should / shouldn't* wait until you're ready to speak. Speak from the beginning!

7. you *should / shouldn't* focus on only one skill. You need to practice listening as well as speaking, writing, and reading.

8. you *should / shouldn't* do a little bit with the language every day, e.g., speak to people, read a book, do some grammar practice, listen to some songs.

3 Complete the postcard with the verbs from the box.

> walk   hear   ~~come~~   meet   learn   eat

Dear Mia,

You should (1) _____**come**_____ to Turkey! It's a fantastic country. We are all having a great time.

I think everyone should (2) _____ a little bit of the language of the place they are visiting. Dad and I spent a couple of weeks learning some Turkish phrases. You should (3) _____ Dad's pronunciation! Everyone laughs, but they really help us! They are really friendly.

One thing: you shouldn't (4) _____ around in the summer without sunblock and a hat. It gets very, very hot! But you should (5) _____ lots and lots of the food. Turkish food is amazing!

We'll be home next week. We should (6) _____ to talk. I want to know all about your trip to Berlin.

Hope you are well.

Love, Frank

Mia Rojas
2 Calle de Guillermo Rolland
28013 Madrid
Spain

Could I ... ? / Do you mind if I ... ?

Could I try on these jeans, please?

Use **Could I ... ?** / **Do you mind if I ... ?** as a polite way of asking someone if you can do something.

Could I try on this T-shirt, please? **Do you mind if I** *try on this hat?*

In formal settings, such as in a store, a common response to questions beginning with **Do you mind ...**
is **Not at all**, but you will also hear **No problem** or **Of course**.

1 **Match the two parts to make questions.**

1 Could you show me where   **a** me later?

2 Do you mind if   **b** the computer room is, please?

3 Could I buy   **c** me how to get to the park?

4 Could you call   **d** I borrow this book?

5 Could you tell   **e** if I try this on?

6 Do you mind   **f** this phone, please?

2 Complete the questions with the words from the box.

> try   if   tell   ~~have~~   mind   Could   Do   show

1 Could I _____have_____ this postcard, please?

2 Do you _____ if I close the window?

3 Could you _____ me your new laptop?

4 _____ I use your phone for a minute, please?

5 _____ you mind if I look at your computer games?

6 Could I _____ on these shoes, please?

7 Could you _____ me where the library is, please?

8 Do you mind _____ I get some milk?

3 Match the questions from Activity 2 with the answers below.

a Of course not. We can play one if you like. _____

b Of course. You're very close. See the tower over there? It's right next door. _____

c Of course. Would you like a stamp as well? ___1___

d Yes. Is yours not working? _____

e Of course. If you need a bigger pair, let me know. _____

f Not at all. It is a little cold in here. _____

g Of course not. The glasses are in the cabinet. _____

h Of course. Just let me finish this email. _____

4 You are visiting a friend's house for the first time. Ask your friend's parents questions using *Could I ... ?* or *Do you mind if I ... ?*

1 Could I have a glass of water, please?

2 _____

3 _____

4 _____

5 _____

6 _____

Reading: A Travel Diary

1 Read the travel diary. Write *t* (true) or *f* (false). Correct the false sentences.

JOE'S TRAVEL DIARY ✈

June 12th

Day One in Seville. What a city! At the hotel, the manager said, "You should be careful. It gets very hot here." I'm glad we listened to him. It was 38 degrees this afternoon. We went for a walk in Maria Luisa Park before dinner, and I had a hat, sunglasses, and a lot of sunblock on. It was so hot!

June 13th

Day Two. We walked all around the old parts of the city today. We lost the map in a café, but it was much more fun when we didn't know where we were going. Dad, Mom, and my sisters took lots of photographs.

June 14th

Day Three in sunny Seville! We went on a boat trip today, down the River Guadalquivir. "Do you mind if we sit here?" Mom asked a family at the front of the boat. They didn't. We spent the day with them. They are from Australia, and today was their last day. We had a good time together.

June 15th

Day Four. A great day! We visited the Alcázar of Seville and the Plaza de España. I practiced my Spanish a lot today. I said, "Could you tell us where the Giralda Tower is, please?" But they didn't understand my Spanish, so I asked again in English!

June 16th

Day Five. Our last day in the city. We all bought souvenirs. Dad bought some plates and a comb, Mom bought a basket, I bought a Spanish flag, and both my sisters bought pajamas. We took a last walk around this afternoon, and then took a taxi to the airport. When we get home, I'm going to say one thing to all of my friends: "You should go to Seville!"

1 On Day One, they bought souvenirs.

    ☐ **f**   They bought souvenirs on Day Five.

2 The family used their cameras a lot on Day Two.

    ☐

3 On Day Three, they met a family from another country.

    ☐

4 They went to the park on Day Four.

    ☐

5 On Day Five, Joe's mom bought a flag.

    ☐

1 **Answer the questions.**

1 Which countries would you like to travel to the most?

_____

2 Who would you like to travel with?

_____

3 What are your favorite things to do when you visit new places?

_____

4 What do you not enjoy doing on trips?

_____

5 What souvenirs do you like to buy when you go to a new place?

_____

Help with Writing

When writing a diary entry, do not include every detail of what happened on a particular day, only the most important details. Create an impression of the day, not a minute-by-minute account of it.

2 **Imagine you are on vacation in one of the following cities:**

- New York
- London
- Paris
- Istanbul
- Madrid
- Beijing

Write a travel diary about the things you have seen and done on your trip. Use Joe's travel diary and your answers to the questions in Activity 1 to help you.

_____

_____

_____

_____

_____

_____

_____

_____

_____

_____

_____

_____

Listening: Souvenirs and Vacations

1 🎧 **13** **Listen and number the pictures.**

a

b

c

d

⬜ **1**

e

⬜

f

⬜

2 🎧 **14** **Listen to the conversations. Complete the sentences with one word.**

1 The girl likes the _____earrings_____ on the wall.
2 The boy wants to buy a _____.
3 The boy doesn't think they should buy their dad a _____.
4 The girl thinks the _____ are expensive.
5 The boy can't see any blue _____ in the store.
6 The girl is going to see other _____ before she buys some.

1 Work with a friend. Imagine you are on vacation in Istanbul. Say which things from the box you should or shouldn't buy and why. Think of more things.

> We should buy a guidebook. It has information about the best sights to see.

a guidebook to Istanbul   T-shirts   sunglasses
a Turkish carpet   a basket   a map of downtown

> I agree. We shouldn't buy …

2 With your friend, look at these tips for a city vacation. Can you correct them?

> We shouldn't only talk to people who speak our language.

> Yes, you're right. We should try to talk to people who speak another language.

On a city vacation …

- only talk to people who speak your language.
- only visit museums.
- eat four ice cream cones a day.
- take 50 photos of the same thing.
- only buy souvenirs.
- always have lunch in your hotel.

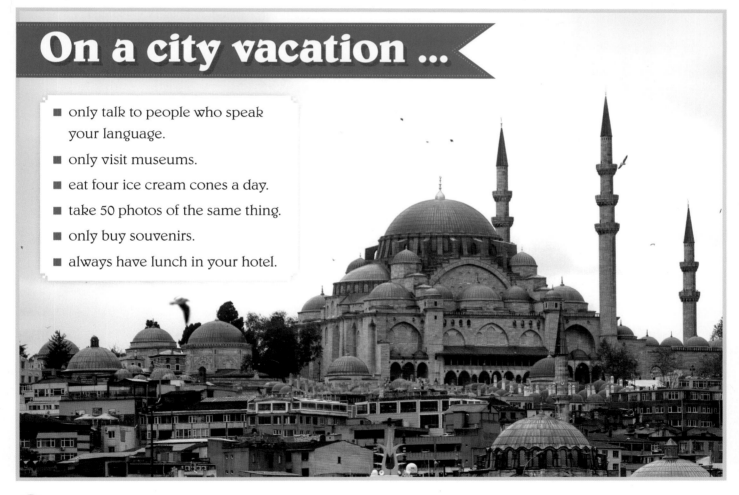

3 With your friend, plan a vacation. Choose a city that you know. Where should you go and what should you do there?

> I think we should go to Valencia.

> Good idea! We should visit …

7 Will for Offers and Promises

I'll help you carry your bags.

SUPERSAVE

Language Focus

We can use **will / 'll** to make offers and promises. **Will / 'll** is followed by the **infinitive without to**.

Offers

*I'm hungry. **I'll make** you a sandwich.*

*That computer looks really heavy. **I'll help** you carry it.*

*I'm thirsty. **I'll get** you a glass of water.*

Promises

*I know I didn't do very well on my tests this time, but **I'll work** hard and do better next time.*

***I'll give** the game back next week.*

***I'll call** you tomorrow.*

1 Correct the underlined parts of the sentences using *will / 'll*.

1 Don't worry, <u>she'll practices</u> every day. She wants to be in the school band.

　she'll practice

2 You look hot. <u>I open</u> the window.

_____

3 Don't worry about the shopping. <u>I'll did</u> it.

_____

4 I promise <u>I'll going</u> to sleep at nine o'clock every night.

_____

5 <u>I'm make</u> lunch when we get home.

_____

6 Don't wait for the bus. <u>I'll took</u> you home.

_____

2 Complete the text with the verbs from the box.

use   wash   do   take   clean   make   ~~stop~~

My friend Alina is always making promises. "I'll **(1)** _____ stop _____ eating so much chocolate," she says. "I'll only **(2)** _____ the internet for one hour every day. I'll **(3)** _____ two hours of homework every night when I come home." "Yes, Alina," I say. At home, she says, "I'll **(4)** _____ up my room every Saturday morning, I'll **(5)** _____ the dishes every night after dinner, and I'll **(6)** _____ Zoom for a walk in the morning before school." Alina really does want to do the things she says, but she finds it much easier to say them than to do them. That's why I said to her, "Alina, will you make me one very special promise?" "Of course!" she said. "I love making promises." "Good," I said. "Make me this promise, then: that you'll never **(7)** _____ any more promises."

3 Circle the correct verb forms to complete the dialogue.

Maggie   Do we **(1)** (know) / *will know* who is bringing what for the picnic tomorrow?

Clare   I'll **(2)** *bring / brought* water and juice.

Daniel   I'll **(3)** *makes / make* some sandwiches tomorrow morning before we go. Cheese and ham, OK?

Maggie   Good idea. I'll **(4)** *baking / bake* a chocolate cake this afternoon.

Daniel   I'll **(5)** *text / texted* Lana and Ceren later to find out if they are coming.

Clare   I'll **(6)** *go / goes* online to check the weather forecast.

Maggie   All right. If it rains, we can have the picnic at my house.

4 Make offers using *will / 'll*.

1 Your dad would like you to help him in the kitchen.

   I'll help him.

2 Your mom says she can't find her keys.

   _____

3 Your sister says it's cold in the house.

   _____

4 Your brother doesn't know how to do his English homework.

   _____

5 Your grandma is tired. She wants some things from the store.

   _____

6 Your best friend's tablet isn't working.

   _____

Present Perfect with *Just*

She's **just scored** a goal.

Use **present perfect** with **just** to talk about something you did a short time ago.

Would you like a sandwich?   *No, thanks. **I've just eaten**.*

Form these phrases in the following way: **has** / **have** + **just** + **past participle**.

***She's just gone** out.*   ***He's just spoken** to them.*

---

1 **Order the words to make sentences.**

1 just / Alicia's / lunch / finished / .   Alicia's just finished lunch.

2 from / work / back / gotten / Mom's / just / .   _____

3 message / text / a / gotten / Paul's / just / .   _____

4 story / heard / just / the / Dad's / .   _____

5 a / just / walk / for / dog / the / Sam's / taken / .   _____

6 test / my / gotten / results / I've / just / .   _____

7 just / home / Tara's / gotten / .   _____

8 history / just / project / her / Sue's / finished / . _____

2 Correct the sentences.

1 I've just saw the photo you sent me. It's really funny!

I've just seen the photo you sent me. It's really funny!

2 Alma just finishing her science homework.

3 Grandma's just get on the bus.

4 Sorry, I just broken the vase.

5 My brother have just seen that movie. He loved it!

6 My sister's just went to bed. She was really tired.

3 Rewrite the sentences with *just* and the present perfect.

1 Jack had a drink a minute ago.   Jack's just had a drink.

2 Mom saw him two minutes ago.

3 Dad and Grandma went out not long ago.

4 I ate something a minute ago.

5 We came back a few minutes ago.

6 My friends heard the news a couple of minutes ago.

4 Write a second sentence with *just* and the present perfect to explain the first sentence.

1 I'm sleepy.

I've just woken up.

2 I'm not thirsty.

3 He's very happy.

4 They're not happy.

5 She's really tired.

6 I'm full.

Reading: A Letter

1   **Read the letter. Order the information.**

Dear Aunt Susan,

I've just received your letter. Thank you for it. I really enjoyed reading it. I will keep writing letters to you, I promise! I know you think I'm going to get bored, but I won't. Lots of my friends talk about how much they want to turn the internet off or put their phones away. I don't think older people know how much younger people like some of the older, slower ways of doing things. Anyway, I will keep writing!

Dad, Mom, and I had a great time on Saturday. We went out to eat at an Italian restaurant, and then we went to the theater. We saw Shakespeare's "A Midsummer Night's Dream." It was fantastic! There were candles all around the stage, and they gave a very special light. There were so many people in the audience! Hundreds and hundreds.

There was a musician playing the lute (What a beautiful instrument!), and he spoke to the audience at the beginning and between the acts. The actors were great. Mom said that actors today sometimes do Shakespeare plays dressed in modern clothes, but these actors were all wearing the kinds of wigs, tights, masks, and costumes of Shakespeare's time.

I was very excited on the way home. I texted all my friends, "I've just seen a great play!" and then I told Mom and Dad that I wanted to be a theater director. When we got home, Dad found a copy of "A Midsummer Night's Dream" on the shelf. I read half of it before I went to bed!

Would you like to come to the next play we see, Aunt Susan?

Write soon.

Best wishes,
Ciaron

a Ciaron texted his friends. ☐

b Ciaron received a letter from his Aunt Susan. ☐ 1

c Ciaron went out to eat. ☐

d Ciaron started reading *A Midsummer Night's Dream*. ☐

e Ciaron told his parents he wanted to be a theater director. ☐

f Ciaron went to the theater. ☐

1 Order the words to make different ways of asking "How are you?"

1 life / is / how / ?   How is life?

2 are / how / things / ?

3 is / everything / how / ?

4 it / how's / going / ?

5 you / doing / are / how / ?

6 you / right / all / everything / with / is / ?

Help with Writing

Digital technology has made letter writing a thing of the past. However, it is still a good alternative to email and text messaging, and it gives you the chance to write at length and practice writing by hand.

2 Imagine you are writing a letter in response to one your relative sent to you. Use Ciaron's letter to help you. Include the following:

- thank your relative for their letter
- say how you are
- give your news
- ask your relative some questions

Listening: At the Theater

1 🎧 **15** **Listen to the conversation. Circle the correct answers.**

1 How many tickets does Lucy want?

    (a) two   **b** three

2 Which Shakespeare play does Lucy want to see?

    a *King Lear*   **b** *Romeo and Juliet*

3 What time does she want to see the play?

    a at 2:30   **b** at 7:30

4 How much are the tickets?

    a $25   **b** $35

5 Who is going to pay for the tickets?

    a Lucy's dad   **b** Lucy's mom

6 What costumes will the actors wear?

    a modern clothes   **b** wigs, tights, and masks from Shakespeare's time

2 🎧 **16** **Listen. Are sentences 1–6 true or false?**

1 Lucy has just arrived at the theater.

2 The play started twenty minutes ago.

3 Tom has just passed the park.

4 Lucy will wait for Tom inside the theater.

5 Tom's sister saw the play on Monday.

6 Tom has just seen one of the actors from the play.

t

1 Work with a friend. Choose one play each. Ask and answer the questions about it.

- What is your play called?
- What is it about?
- What time does it start?
- How much are the tickets?

 Stratfordtheater.com 🔍

The Mask of Antaro When a theater director sees Antaro wearing an old mask, he gives him a part in his new play. But Antaro is a terrible actor. Will he tell the director his secret? This comedy is playing for three weeks.
Starts at 7:00. **Tickets:** $10

Victoria's Albert Victoria was queen of the U.K. from 1837 to 1901. This history play tells us about the queen's love for her husband, Prince Albert. He died in 1861 when he was 42. See *Victoria's Albert* until the end of December.
Starts at 7:30. **Tickets:** $12

The Last Sword Whoever takes the last sword from the Castle of Muldeen will become the strongest person in the world. But what will be lost by those who fight to get the sword? This tragedy is playing for two weeks.
Starts at 6:45. **Tickets:** $15

Help with Speaking

When you are speaking, if you want to use a word but don't know what it is in English, try to describe it. Maybe your friend knows it!

2 With your friend, choose a play from Activity 1 that you want to see. Make arrangements. Talk about:

- what you are going to see
- who is going to buy the tickets
- where you are going to meet
- when you are going to meet

> Let's see *The Last Sword*. It sounds great. I like tragedies. What about you?

> I think *The Last Sword* is a good idea. I'll buy the tickets.

3 Work with a different friend. Talk about your plans from Activity 2.

> On Saturday, Yusuf and I are going to see *The Last Sword*. Yusuf is going to buy the tickets, and I …

8 First Conditional

Come on, Jon. **If we study** hard, **we'll do** well on the test.

Language Focus

Use **if clauses** to talk about something that is a possibility in the future.

If I finish my homework in time, I'll go to the movies.

This kind of conditional sentence is called the **first conditional**, and we use it to say that when one thing happens, another thing becomes a possibility. These sentences are formed in the following way:

If + **simple present** + **will** + **infinitive without to**

1 Match the two parts of the sentences.

1 If we have robots in our homes,   a I'll teach you some chords.
2 If you want to learn to play piano,   b we'll go out on our sled.
3 If you're hungry,   c our lives will be easier.
4 If you want to go to the concert,   d I'll buy the tickets this afternoon.
5 If it snows,   e we'll visit the Hagia Sophia.
6 If we go to Istanbul,   f I'll make you something to eat.

2 Circle the correct verb forms to complete the text.

I like thinking about the future. You know, if this happens, that will **(1)** *happen* / *happens*. Well, maybe it won't happen, but I like dreaming about things. If I **(2)** *will go* / *go* to college one day, I'll meet lots of people. And if I **(3)** *meets* / *meet* lots of people, I'll go to lots of places with them. And if I go to lots of places with them, I **(4)** *learn* / *will learn* all about the world. And if I learn all about the world, I'll **(5)** *understand* / *understood* things better than I do now. I think like that, you see. But when I stop, I wonder if it's true. Maybe it's not a great idea to spend all your time dreaming about the future. But if I don't do that, what will I **(6)** *do* / *doing*?

3 Complete the dialogue with the verbs from the box in the correct form.

> do   rain   be (x2)   ~~go~~   dance   plan   see

Mira   What are we going to do this summer?

Sami   Lots of things! If it's hot, we'll **(1)** _____go_____ to Las Palmas Beach.

Mira   And if it **(2)** _____ too busy there, we'll go to the Arco Iris Pool.

Sami   Great idea! And if there **(3)**_____ too many people there, we'll go to the park.

Mira   If we go to the park, we'll **(4)** _____ The Rockets. They're playing at the music festival this year.

Sami   Oh, yes!

Mira   And if we see The Rockets, we'll **(5)** _____ all afternoon.

Sami   We will! I love their music.

Mira   If it's rainy, what will we **(6)**_____?

Sami   Good question. Read? Watch TV? Go online?

Mira   I know. If it **(7)** _____ , we'll **(8)** _____ next summer!

4 Complete the sentences using *will* / *'ll*.

My Summer Vacation Plans

1   If it rains, **we'll go to the movies.** _____

2   If it's sunny, _____

3   If I visit my cousins, _____

4   If we go on vacation, _____

5   If I stay at my grandparents' house, _____

6   If we stay at home, _____

What if ... ?

Let's go to the pool.

What if it's closed?

Use **What if ... ?** to ask someone what will happen in the future as a consequence of another thing happening.

*I'm looking forward to going to the beach on Saturday, but **what if** it rains?*

1 Make questions.

1 late / we're / if / what / ?   What if we're late?

2 snows / what / it / if / ?

3 computer / breaks / the / if / what / ?

4 at / if / home / not / what / they're / ?

5 pass / test / don't / we / what / the / if / ?

6 the / don't / have / if / what / one / they / right / ?

70

2 Match the questions with the answers.

1 What if it rains?
2 What if we don't have any bread?
3 What if we miss the bus?
4 What if Jon's out?
5 What if there are no tickets left?
6 What if we lose the game?

a We won't! We have the best team!
b Don't worry. We'll take an umbrella.
c We'll catch the train.
d We'll watch the concert online.
e I'll go to the store.
f We'll call him.

3 Complete the dialogues with the words from the box.

do   he   go   if   What   ~~like~~

1 **Lou**   Let's have a surprise party for Sena's birthday.
  Mika   What if she doesn't _____**like**_____ it?
  Lou   Of course she will. She loves surprises!
2 **Rachel** Let's go to see that show at the Old Theater.
  Selin   _____ if it isn't very good?
  Rachel We'll leave at intermission!
3 **Li**   Let's go to the movies this afternoon.
  Lucia   What _____ nothing's playing?
  Li   Don't worry. We'll do something else.
4 **David**   Let's go over to Hal's house.
  Kadir   What if _____ isn't there?
  David   We'll go to see Elena.
5 **Mark**   Let's finish that math homework.
  Paul   What if we can't _____ it?
  Mark   I'll ask my sister to help us.
6 **Carmen** Let's go to that new café for dessert.
  Chan   What if the desserts aren't very good?
  Carmen We'll _____ to a different café!

4 Write questions with *What if*.

1 Let's go to the park.   What if it's closed?
2 Let's make a pizza.   _____
3 Let's play tennis.   _____
4 Let's play computer games.   _____
5 Let's go to the beach.   _____

Reading: A Newspaper Article

1 Read the newspaper article. Complete the sentences.

The Weekly Report | April 10th

NEWS \\ ROBOTS OF THE FUTURE

The Cyborg Factory in Berlin makes robots. Right now, they are very expensive to produce and very expensive to buy, but Helga Weber, the factory's chief engineer, believes we are at the beginning of a consumer revolution. "If you believe what all the experts say," she says, "in the future, robots will be everywhere. They will be cheaper to make and buy. These robots will do many of the things that people do now. If you have a problem with your teeth, for example, you'll go to a robot dentist who will be programmed to check your teeth and tell you if they are OK. Robot cleaners will clean our houses, while robot engineers will design and build the world around us."

Right now, the Cyborg Factory only manufactures robot mechanics for the car industry, but things are beginning to change. "We're working on a design for robot farmers right now. The demand is growing in the world of agriculture for robots who can be programmed to do the same task again and again."

The factory is impressive. It's on an enormous site in western Berlin and employs over 2,000 people. Will all of these people have jobs in the future? Helga laughs. "Who knows?" she says. "Maybe we will all be replaced. My colleagues think there will be robot businessmen and -women, robot computer programmers, and even robot artists and robot police officers." Thankfully, in the course of our conversation, Helga did not say whether there would ever be robot journalists.

1 The company is called the Cyborg _____**Factory**_____ .

2 It is located in _____ .

3 Helga Weber is the chief _____ .

4 The company produces only robot _____ right now.

5 Right now, it is working on a design for robot _____ .

6 Over _____ people work for the company.

1 Complete the table with the information from the box.

> Tokyo, Japan   ~~Robots for Art~~   robot artists   Kondo Taka
> multinational companies, rich businessmen and -women
> "If you tell the robot what kind of painting you want, it will do exactly what you ask."

Name of the Company	Robots for Art
Location	
What It Produces	
Who Buys the Robots?	
Name of the Chief Engineer	
What the Chief Engineer Says	

Help with Writing

When writing an article, put the most important information at the very beginning. You should not make readers wait long to find out exactly what the feature is about.

2 Imagine you write for the newspaper *The Weekly Report*. Write an article about Robots for Art using the notes you made in Activity 1 and the article on the Reading page to help you. Include the following information:

- a title for the newspaper article
- the name and location of the company
- what the robots can do and who buys them
- who the chief engineer is and what she says

_____

_____

_____

_____

Listening: The Robot Exhibition

1 🎧 **17** **Listen to the conversation at a robot exhibition. Answer the questions.**

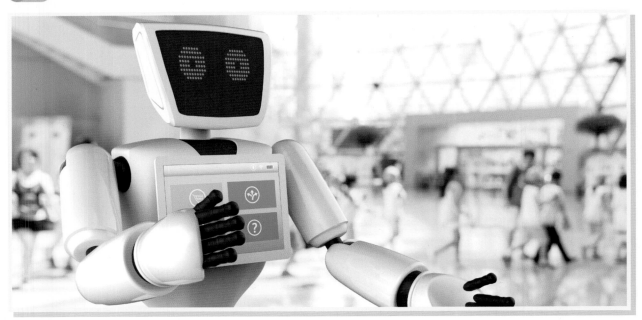

1 What does Holly's mom do?

She's an engineer.

2 What does Holly's dad do?

_____

3 What does Holly want to be?

_____

4 What does Greg want to be?

_____

5 What is the exhibition called?

_____

6 Where can you press buttons on the robots?

_____

2 🎧 **18** **Listen. Complete the instructions on how to use the robot.**

⚙ HOW TO USE THE 28QAZ

You can call her **(1)** _____Betty_____.
If you press the purple button, she will
(2) _____ and **(3)** _____
the dishes for you.
She will become an **(4)** _____ if
you press the pink button.
If you press the black button, she will be your
car **(5)** _____.
If you want to turn off your robot, press the
(6) _____ button.

1 **Talk about the robot. Play the guessing game.**

> If you press this button, the robot will do your homework.

> It's the blue button.

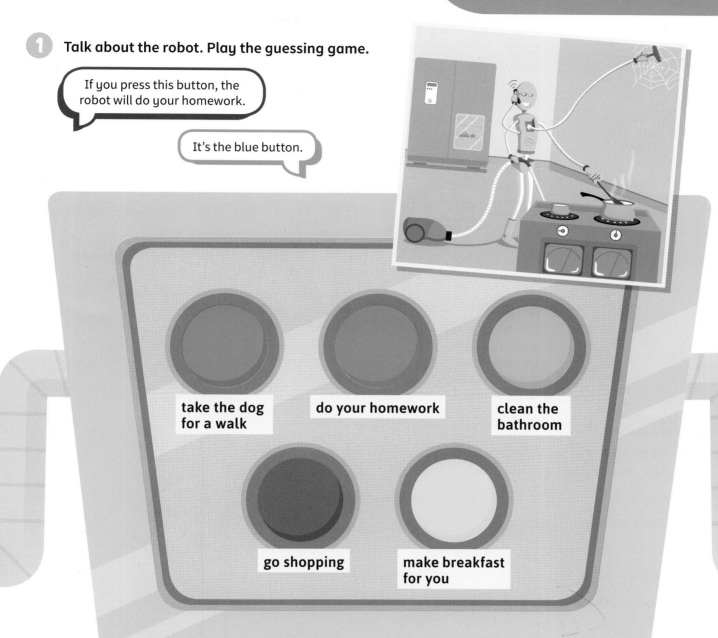

take the dog for a walk

do your homework

clean the bathroom

go shopping

make breakfast for you

2 **Work with a friend. Look at the jobs in the box. Imagine that robots will do these jobs in the future. Ask and answer.**

> What if there are robot house cleaners in the future?

house cleaner   mechanic   dentist   farmer   teacher   doctor

> If there are robot house cleaners, people won't …

3 **Work with a different friend. Talk about your ideas in Activity 2. Are any of them the same?**

> Maria and I think that if there are robot house cleaners, people won't have to clean their homes anymore. They will have more time to do other things.

Present Perfect with Already and Yet

My sister loves traveling. **She's already been** to Egypt, Turkey, the U.S.A., Kenya, the U.K., Spain, Italy, and Australia. Amazing!

Language Focus

Use **present perfect** with **already** to talk about actions that have happened before now. **Already** means "before now" or "before this time."

This is the form of the sentence: **has / have** + **already** + **past participle**

I've already seen the new Star Wars *movie.*

Already is also used to express surprise that something has happened so soon.

*Jane is only ten, but she has **already** won twenty swim competitions.*

Use **present perfect** with **yet** to talk about actions that haven't happened up to now. **Yet** means "up to now" or "up to this moment in time."

This is the form of the sentence: **hasn't / haven't** + **past participle** + **yet**

I haven't seen the new Star Wars *movie **yet**.*

---

1 Write the past participles.

1 be	**been**	**6** make	
2 go		**7** write	
3 do		**8** read	
4 have		**9** learn	
5 see		**10** eat	

2 Complete the sentences with the past participles from Activity 1 and *yet* or *already*.

1 My parents have traveled all over the world, but they haven't ____**been**____ to New Zealand ____**yet**____ .

2 Neil is incredible! He's _____ _____ English, Spanish, Chinese, and Arabic.

3 What a week! We've _____ _____ tests in French, geography, and science.

4 I haven't _____ the cake _____ . Would you like to help me?

5 I don't want anything, thanks. I've _____ _____ lunch.

6 Joby's _____ _____ out. He decided to go earlier than planned.

7 I haven't _____ that new cartoon about pirates _____ .

8 Hannah's _____ _____ half of her story for English class.

9 Sorry, I can't come to the park now. I haven't _____ my homework _____ .

10 I've just finished reading *The Lord of the Rings* trilogy, but my sister hasn't _____ the first book _____ .

3 Complete the text with the verbs from the box in the correct form and *yet* or *already*.

> think   go   write   break   read   ~~have~~

Mr. Hannon said, "Write about your experiences for homework." I said, "Mr. Hannon, I'm only twelve. I don't think I've **(1)** ____**had**____ any experiences ____**yet**____ ." Mr. Hannon laughed. "Of course you have," he said. "Think about it."

I've **(2)** _____ about it, and I guess I have had some experiences. For example, I've **(3)** _____ my right leg twice, but I hope I don't do it a third time. Oh, and I've **(4)** _____ to the moon. I went last Wednesday, but only in a dream.

I've **(5)** _____ 114 books (yes, I am counting). I've **(6)** _____ four stories about a sad mouse named Richard, and the local newspaper has published them all. "Well," said Mr. Hannon when I showed him my homework. "You see? You've already experienced a lot. You just had to think about it."

4 Write about your experiences.

1 I've already _____ .

2 I've already _____ .

3 I've already _____ .

4 I've already _____ .

5 I haven't _____ yet.

6 I haven't _____ yet.

7 I haven't _____ yet.

8 I haven't _____ yet.

Have you ... yet?

Have you finished your homework **yet**, Orla? We're going to have dinner soon.

Language Focus

Use **Have you ... yet?** to ask someone if they have done something at some point up to now.

Have you finished your history project **yet?**

1 Make questions.

1 that / yet / you / read / have / book / ?

   Have you read that book yet?

2 the / movie / yet / have / you / seen / ?

   _____

3 yet / song / heard / that / you / have / ?

   _____

4 Chinese / your / yet / you / have / lessons / started / ?

   _____

5 anything / you / have / had / to / yet / eat / ?

   _____

6 card / yet / a / Dad / bought / birthday / have / you / ?

   _____

7 that / game / played / yet / new / computer / you / have / ?

   _____

8 you / kitchen / cleaned / the / have / yet / ?

   _____

2 Complete the questions with the verbs from the box in the correct form.

> go · walk · ~~feed~~ · wash · do · call · clean · make

1 Have you _____**fed**_____ the cat yet?

2 Have you _____ your English project yet?

3 Have you _____ shopping yet?

4 Have you _____ breakfast yet?

5 Have you _____ the dishes yet?

6 Have you _____ the dog yet?

7 Have you _____ your room yet?

8 Have you _____ your sister yet?

3 Match the answers with the questions from Activity 2.

a Yes, I have. I've put everything away! _____

b Yes, I have. Come down. Your toast is getting cold! _____

c No, I haven't. I'll do them now. _____

d Yes, I have. But she didn't answer. _____

e Yes, I have. Haven't you seen her? She's covered in mud! _____

f No, I haven't. I'm going to the store after lunch. _____

g Yes, I have. He was so hungry, he jumped up at me! __1__

h No, I haven't. It's very hard. I'm going to talk to Mom about it later. _____

4 Complete the text with *have*, *haven't*, *already*, and *yet*.

My mom and dad ask me the same questions
every day. They begin,
(1) " _____**Have**_____ you" and finish
with (2) "_____?" The usual
one is, (3) "_____ you cleaned
your room (4) _____?"
but their second favorite question is,
(5) "_____ you done your
homework (6) _____?"
My usual answer is, "No, I
(7) _____," but sometimes
I say, "Yes, I (8) _____,"
and then they are very happy with me.

Reading: A Postcard

1 Read the postcard. Write *t* (true) or *f* (false). Correct the false sentences.

Dear Mom and Dad,

Day three! We've already been to Buckingham Palace, Tower Bridge, and the British Museum.

Yesterday we went to the National Maritime Museum! It's enormous! We saw old sails and masts and thousands of model ships with beautiful portholes and lifeboats. The exhibit I was most interested in were the barometers. Did you know that sailors began to use them in the 18th century?

Tomorrow, we're going on the London Eye!

Love,

Gareth

Mr. and Mrs. Thomas
52 Park Street
Cardiff
South Wales
CF10 INS
U.K.

1 Gareth is on the third day of his trip.

  [t] _____

2 Gareth hasn't been to Buckingham Palace yet.

  [ ] _____

3 Gareth's already been to the British Museum.

  [ ] _____

4 Gareth has already been to Tower Bridge.

  [ ] _____

5 Gareth didn't see the barometers at the National Maritime Museum.

  [ ] _____

6 Gareth hasn't been on the London Eye yet.

  [ ] _____

1 Match 1–5 with a–e to make common ways of signing off a postcard.

1 With
2 Lots
3 Love
4 Wish you
5 Best

a of love,
b wishes,
c were here,
d from,
e love,

Help with Writing

Postcards tend to follow a certain structure: we say where we are, what we have done, what we are going to do, and then we sign off.

2 Imagine that you are on a trip to London with your school. Write a postcard to your parents. Tell them about your trip. Use Gareth's postcard to help you. Include the following information:

- what you have already seen and done
- what you haven't done yet

Listening: On Board Ship

1 🎧 **19** Listen to the conversation. Complete the sentences.

1 The ship where Eve and her dad are is a _____museum_____.
2 Eve and her dad can see where the _____ stood.
3 When sailors sailed the ship, there were _____ on board.
4 Eve and her dad have already seen the _____, the _____, and the old _____.
5 Now they are going to find the _____.
6 Eve's dad sees a rat under the _____, but it's made of plastic.

2 🎧 **20** Listen to the conversation. Circle the correct words and phrases.

1 There *will* / *won't* be stores on board.
2 Robert *has already packed his clothes* / *hasn't packed his clothes yet*.
3 Robert *hasn't put any* / *has put some* ebooks on his phone.
4 Robert's mom *has already been on a ship* / *hasn't been on a ship yet*.
5 Robert's grandpa was a sailor for *twenty years* / *more than twenty years*.
6 Robert's *grandpa* / *dad* visited thirty-five countries.

1 Talk about the captain. Play the memory game.

> Has Mary May visited India yet?

> Yes, she has.

> How many times has she been to India?

> She's been to India ten times.

⚓ THE ANCHOR JUNE ISSUE

SAILOR OF THE MONTH
Captain Mary May, from Scotland

Countries Visited	Countries Not Visited
India (ten times)	Egypt
Turkey (five times)	Mexico
Australia (three times)	China
Argentina (twice)	Colombia

2 Draw a picture of a captain. Complete and practice.

This is Captain _____.
He's/She's from _____.
He's/She's _____ years old and has already visited many countries.
He's/She's been to _____, _____, and _____. He/She hasn't visited
_____, _____, or _____ yet.

3 Talk about your captain.

> This is Captain Jack Smith. He's from the U.S.A. He's thirty-five years old, and …

Audioscripts

01

Ms. Bell	OK, class. We're going to do some experiments today. Let's get the things that we need. Where are the goggles?
Jane	They were on the shelf yesterday, Ms. Bell. We didn't need them.
Ms. Bell	Ah, right. There they are. Thank you, Jane. Now, the test tubes. Did you use them with Mr. White yesterday?
Boy	No, we didn't.
Ms. Bell	OK. So the test tubes are in the cabinet. What about the aprons?
Jane	We put the aprons back in the drawer after yesterday's experiment.
Ms. Bell	Great! You are a neat class! OK, so that's goggles, test tubes, and aprons. Now, what's next … Let's see … Oh, yes – gloves!
Boy	We threw them away yesterday, Ms. Bell. They're in the trash can. We need new gloves.
Ms. Bell	Yes, of course. Let's get new gloves then. And the last thing is the instructions for today's experiment. Hmm … Where did I put them?
Samantha	Um … Ms. Bell?
Ms. Bell	Yes, Samantha?
Samantha	You're holding them.
Ms. Bell	Am I? Oh, yes. Here they are! Thank you. Now, look at my desk, everyone. Can you see this blue liquid here? Well, we're going to …

02

1

Mom	How was your day, Max?
Max	It was … um … interesting.
Mom	Why? What happened?
Max	Well, we did an experiment with Ms. Bell, and it went wrong. There was an explosion.
Mom	An explosion?!
Max	Don't worry, Mom. It was only a small one!

2

Jill	Dad, where did you put my book?
Dad	Which book, Jill?
Jill	My science book. We have a test tomorrow.
Dad	Oh, I put it on the shelf in your room. Next to your desk.
Jill	Great! Thanks, Dad.

3

Man	Hi, Jack. How was the science test?
Jack	It wasn't easy.
Man	Well, science can be a difficult subject.
Jack	Well, the science tests are always difficult, but I think I did OK on this one. There were lots of questions about Isaac Newton, and I knew the answers.
Man	Good job!

4

George	Hello, Sophie. Did you watch the movie last night?
Sophie	The one about the scientist? Yes, I watched it. It was great! Did you like it, George?
George	Not really.
Sophie	Oh! Why not?
George	Well, I thought it was a little boring.

5

Katy	Hi, Oscar. How was your weekend?
Oscar	Really good; thanks, Katy. How was yours?
Katy	Mine was good, too, but we didn't go to the Science Museum after all.
Oscar	Oh! Why not?
Katy	My parents were busy. What did you do this weekend, Oscar?
Oscar	I went to the Science Museum!
Katy	Really!?

6

Dad	Hi, Helen! You look happy.
Helen	I am, Dad!
Dad	Why?
Helen	Mr. Mason liked my project!
Dad	The math one?
Helen	No, the science one. We did the math project last week.

03

Teacher	OK, Leo. It's your turn. Please tell us the story about your grandpa.
Leo	My grandpa's story is incredible. He was in the middle of a natural disaster! It was 1980, and Grandpa was working in the U.S.A. He was a young man then. He was only twenty. Grandpa was living in the state of Washington. He was working near a volcano called Mount St. Helens. While Grandpa was working there, he became interested in the volcano. He thought it was going to erupt again. For months before the eruption, there were lots of earthquakes! But when Mount St. Helens finally erupted, it was still a shock. When it happened, Grandpa was in his car. He heard the loud noise, stopped the car, and looked behind him. In the distance, he saw the smoke rising into the air. He took one photo, and then got back in his car and drove away. Lots of people died that day, but my grandpa was very lucky. I hope I'm never near a volcano when one erupts!

04

Hello! Guess what? This weekend, I lived through an earthquake! Yes, that's right—an earthquake. On Saturday, I went to my town's new museum. It's full of objects from Greek and Roman history. I went there with my family—Mom, Dad, and my brother Henry. We were having a great time. We saw old statues from 2,000 years ago! There were beautiful columns from an ancient Greek temple, too. There was a lot to enjoy. Then, I remember I was taking a photo of a Greek fountain when suddenly the earth started moving! "It's an earthquake!" Mom shouted. "Quick! Run!" We all ran to the corner of the room, and everyone covered their heads with their arms. Vases—lots of vases—were falling to the floor on the other side of the room! We were very scared. But just when the lights went out, the shaking stopped. It was over!

05

Lily	Hey, Ben. Look at these amazing facts! Did you know that it rains a lot in the Amazon rainforest?
Ben	Well, that's why it's called a rainforest, Lily!
Lily	Ha ha, that's true. Well, it says here that every year the Amazon rainforest gets between 1,500 and 3,000 millimeters of rain!
Ben	Between 1,500 and 3,000 millimeters? That is a lot of water!
Lily	Look at this photo, Ben. This tree is a bristlecone pine tree. It's in the White Mountains of California.
Ben	In the U.S.A.?
Lily	That's right. How old is the oldest tree of this kind? Take a guess!
Ben	Hmm … I don't know … 500 years old?
Lily	Much older! More than 4,800 years old!
Ben	Wow! That's almost 5,000! Amazing!
Lily	Do you know the green anaconda?
Ben	Yes, it's a snake. They live in South America.
Lily	That's right. It can weigh around 227 kilograms!
Ben	227 kilos? That's a heavy snake!
Lily	This fact is incredible.
Ben	Tell me.

Lily Did you know that there are about 400,000 kinds of beetles?

Ben I can't believe it. Does it say 400 or 40,000?

Lily 400,000. That's one quarter of all the animal species in the world!

Ben Oh, look—spider monkeys. They're great! What does it say about them?

Lily They have really long tails. They use them to climb from tree to tree.

Ben How long are their tails?

Lily They can be up to 90 centimeters long. That's almost one meter!

Ben Wow!

Lily OK. Here's the last fact. You know there are millions of ants in the Amazon rainforest?

Ben Yes. Well, ants are everywhere!

Lily That's right. Now, how many different kinds of ants are there in the world?

Ben Um … 10,000?

Lily You were close! 12,000. There are 12,000 different kinds of ants.

Ben That's a lot! I don't like ants!

 06

Dad Come on, Alex! It's time to get up! We have to do lots of things.

Alex Oh, can I stay in bed a little, Dad? What time is it?

Dad It's time to pack, Alex. We're flying to Brazil later today. Remember?

Alex OK. What do we have to do?

Dad First, you have to pack your things. After that, you have to take a shower and get dressed.

Alex OK. What about breakfast?

Dad I have to make breakfast. We're going to have it just before we go.

Alex Sounds good. Oh, Dad, do I have to take my boots with me?

Dad Yes, good thinking. We need boots for the jungle. Listen, Alex. After breakfast, Mom and I have to pack the car. Can you wash the dishes and dry them, please?

Alex Dad!

Dad Come on, Alex!

Alex OK. I can do that. But do I also have to clean my room before we go?

Dad No. You don't have to clean your room.

Alex Great! Thanks, Dad!

Unit 3 page 34

 07

Cass With me on *Music Hour* today is the singer Chris Frank. Hi, Chris.

Chris Hi, Cass. Thanks for having me on the show.

Cass It's my pleasure! Now, we asked your fans to send us some questions for you. They sent us hundreds! Here's the first one: when are you going to start recording your new album?

Chris Next week!

Cass That's very soon! Do you have a name for your album?

Chris Yes, it's *Spotlight*. It's going to be a different music genre this time: jazz!

Cass Jazz is different! OK. Another question: are you going to do anything new this year?

Chris Yes! I'm going to learn to play the bass guitar, Cass.

Cass Sounds great! You can play the bass guitar on your next album! OK. I have two more questions here: when you're not on tour, what time do you usually get up?

Chris Ha! Very late! I usually get up at about twenty past nine!

Cass And what time do you go to bed?

Chris Hmm … I don't go to bed late when I'm not on tour. At half past eleven, usually.

Cass That's late, Chris!

Chris Not for me, Cass. When I'm on tour, I go to bed at about two o'clock in the morning!

08

Daisy Are you going to the concert on Saturday, Jake?

Jake Yes, I am, Daisy. But I don't know how I'm going to get there.

Daisy My dad is going to drive my sister and me. Would you like to come with us?

Jake Yes, please!

Daisy Great! We're going to leave at twenty to six, so come to my house at five-thirty.

Jake OK! What time does the show start?

Daisy At quarter past seven. Do you want to go for pizza before it starts? My sister wants to do that.

Jake Can we get pizza at the theater, then?

Daisy Yes, there are going to be lots of food stalls outside.

Jake Sounds great!

Daisy I know. Hey, guess what? I know someone in the band.

Jake Really?

Daisy Yes. My cousin. She's one of the backup singers.

Jake That's amazing!

Daisy She wants me to go on the stage and be one of the dancers!

Jake No way! Are you going to do it?

Daisy No, I'm not!

Jake Oh, come on, Daisy. You are a rock star!

Unit 4 page 42

09

My grandma tells me that when she was young, only astronauts went into space. Everything's different now! Last summer, I went into space for the weekend with my family. It was our third time! We stayed at the Galaxy Space Hotel, near the moon. It's an amazing place! We arrived at the hotel on Friday, July 31st. This was a special day for me; it was my birthday! That night, we had dinner in the hotel's restaurant. It's called Cosmic, and I love it. All the waiters there are robots! For dinner, we had the "Cosmic space menu." The food was delicious! The day after my birthday, Saturday, August 1st, we went for a spacewalk. Then we had a pizza candy for lunch. That was the last pizza candy that I had. In the evening, we looked at the stars. On Sunday, August 2nd, we came back home. It was a very short trip, but do you know what? We're going back in December for my dad's birthday!

10

These days, tourists often come to space to try "space food." Many go to the Cosmic restaurant at the Galaxy Space Hotel. If you choose Cosmic, you eat candy that tastes like real food. You don't need salt or pepper. And there aren't any napkins, knives, forks, or spoons. You just have to put a piece of candy in your mouth. Yes, a piece of candy! "Wow," people say. "This candy tastes just like a hamburger!" Yes, people like Cosmic, but … we think they're going to enjoy Solar even more. Solar is the newest restaurant in space, and it opens on Saturday, May 3rd. If you like real food, come to Solar. Really, who wants to eat a chicken sandwich in a candy when you can eat a real chicken sandwich? There's another problem with Cosmic, of course. If you eat your dinner in a candy, you finish it in one minute. Here at Solar, we like to take our time and enjoy our food. After all, we have the best view in the universe! What are you waiting for? Give us a call and reserve your table at Solar now! If you reserve a table before April 30th, you get a free space strawberry milkshake. The Solar experience is different. Why don't you come and try it?

Unit 5 page 50

 11

In the days of the old West, in the town of Random Creek, there were two sheriffs: Big John Warren and Bison Bill. They both wanted to be the most important person around, so Big John Warren and Bison Bill always made sure they looked different. John wore boots made of brown leather. Bill wore boots made of black leather. John's scarf was blue; Bill's scarf was red. Of course, both men had a pistol, which they kept in a holster, but John's holster was made of gray leather, while Bill's holster was made of brown leather. Even their hats were different. Bill's was yellow; John's was white. Now, Big John Warren and Bison Bill's job was to catch robbers and send them to jail. But Random Creek's jails were always empty. Do you know why? Well, Big John Warren and Bison Bill spent all their time thinking about how they could be better than each other! While Big John Warren chose a silver badge and Bison Bill chose a golden one, the robbers stole from the good people of Random Creek, and they got away with it!

 12

It was a cold night in Silver Town and Bella Three-Trees, the famous robber, was standing at the edge of the town. Dressed like the night, from her black leather boots to her black leather hat, she was ready to steal again. She took a bottle tied to her saddle and drank from it. The bottle had cold black coffee in it, her favorite. "That's better," she said, wiping her mouth on her shirt sleeve. Then she patted her new horse and said, "Let's go rob people." Now, the other robbers of Silver Town were very good. They rode in on their horses and stole things before the sheriffs knew they were there. The robbers' horses were quick, you see. But Bella Three-Trees was the best robber around. She used a piece of rope with a loop at the end. She threw it over something that she wanted to steal, and then pulled it back to her. Bella stole bottles made of glass and pistols made of metal. But that night in Silver Town, everything went wrong. Outside the jail, Bella's horse raised up on her back legs, and Bella fell to the ground. Lights went on in the jailhouse. Sheriff Cat B. Thompson walked outside. "Well, well, well," she said. "Look who it is. I have a nice cell for you in jail, Bella. But before I take you there, I'm going to feed my horse, Gray Shelly. This isn't Random Creek," said Sheriff Thompson. "We know just how to catch robbers here in Silver Town."

Unit 6 page 58

 13

1 **Charlie** This market is fantastic, Alice!

  Alice I know! I love Istanbul!

  Charlie Me, too. Oh, look what's over there!

  Alice Earrings! Great! I need some new earrings.

2 **Alice** Charlie! Come over here. Look at this carpet.

Charlie Wow! It's amazing! It's the perfect carpet for our living room. Should we ask Mom and Dad to buy it?

  Alice Well, it's very expensive … OK, let's ask them.

3 **Charlie** Alice, could you help me, please?

  Alice Yes, of course.

  Charlie I can't reach that basket on the wall. Could you get it, please?

  Alice Yes, there you go. It's a pretty basket!

  Charlie Yes. Thanks, Alice!

4 **Alice** Mmm … What a nice smell!

  Charlie What are you talking about, Alice?

  Alice The soap at this stall. Can't you smell it?

  Charlie Oh, yes. But I don't think it smells very nice!

5 **Alice** Look at this, Charlie. Do you like it?

  Charlie Yes, it's a beautiful plate.

  Alice I want to buy it!

  Charlie Hmm … You shouldn't buy a plate. What are you going to use it for?

  Alice For my lunch!

6 **Charlie** How about this one, Alice?

  Alice Really?

  Charlie Don't you like it?

  Alice I prefer this pillow, Charlie. What do you think?

 14

1 **Man** Good morning. Can I help you?

  Girl Yes, please. Could I see those earrings on the wall?

  Man Yes, of course. One minute, please.

2 **Boy** Do you mind if I ask you a question?

  Woman Not at all. How can I help you?

  Boy Are these the only flags you have?

  Woman Oh, no! We have a lot more flags. Come this way.

3 **Grace** Peter, what about this for Dad?

  Peter Are you joking, Grace?

  Grace Of course not. It's the most beautiful comb in the market.

  Peter Yes, it's very nice. But Dad doesn't have any hair!

4 **Girl** Hello. Could I try these on, please?

  Man Yes, of course. Here you go.

  Girl They look great. But they're expensive. Do you have any other pairs?

  Man No, I'm sorry. They are the only sunglasses in the store.

5 **Boy** Excuse me. Do you mind if I pick this up?

  Man Not at all. But please be careful with it.

  Boy Yes, of course.

  Man Do you like it?

  Boy Yes, I do. But I'd like a blue one.

  Man No problem. I'll check if we have any blue cups.

6 **Girl** Could I buy these ones, please?

  Woman Yes, of course. But these aren't the only ones in the store.

  Girl Really?

  Woman There are more rings in the other room. Would you like to see them before you buy these?

  Girl Yes, sure!

Unit 7 page 66

 15

John Hello, Stratford Theater. This is John speaking. How can I help you?

Girl Good morning. I'd like to buy two tickets for *Romeo and Juliet*, please. We've just tried to buy them on your website, but it didn't work.

John Oh, don't worry. I'll help you. Which day would you like to see *King Lear*?

Girl I want to see *Romeo and Juliet*.

John Oh, I'm sorry. We have both shows playing right now. When would you like to see *Romeo and Juliet*?

Girl This Saturday.

John At half past two?

Girl No, at half past seven, please.

John OK. I'll check if we have any tickets left. One minute … Let me see … Yes, we have some tickets left. And you wanted two, right?

Girl Yes, that's right.

John OK. That'll be $25 then, please. I'll need some credit card information. Could I talk to your mom or dad?

Girl Of course. My dad's going to pay for the tickets. Oh, but I have a question: will the actors wear modern costumes?

John No, they won't. They'll wear wigs, tights, and special masks exactly like in Shakespeare's time. You'll love it!

Girl It sounds amazing! Thanks for your help. I'll get my dad now. Dad! I've just ordered the tickets!

 16

Lucy Hello … Tom? Can you hear me?

Tom Yes, hi, Lucy.

Lucy I've just arrived at the theater. Where are you?

Tom I'm on the bus.

Lucy You're joking! Tom, the play starts in twenty minutes!

Tom Don't worry. I'll be there. We're not far away.

Lucy Are you sure?

Tom Yes, we've just passed the park, so we should be there in about five minutes. Where should I meet you?

Lucy Hmm … I'll wait inside, next to the place where you can buy snacks and drinks.

Tom OK. I'll see you there soon!

Lucy Great. I can't wait to see the play, Tom!

Tom It'll be amazing. My sister loved it.

Lucy When did she see it?

Tom On Monday. She went with my mom.

Lucy I don't believe it!

Tom She did! They went on …

Lucy No, I mean I've just seen one of the actors from the play.

Tom Really? Who?

Lucy It's Romeo. I don't know his real name. He's wearing tights and a wig. He's talking to some people in the corner.

Tom Why don't you say hello to him?

Lucy Yes! And I'll ask him for a selfie!

Unit 8 page 74

 17

Greg What do you want to do when you're older, Holly? Do you want to be an engineer like your mom? Or a computer programmer like your dad?

Holly Hmm … well, I don't want to be an engineer or a computer programmer. I'd like to be a businesswoman.

Greg A businesswoman?

Holly Yes. I have an idea for my own company.

Greg What is it?

Holly I can't tell you yet!

Greg Oh, come on, Holly, please!

Holly No, you'll have to wait. But what about you, Greg? Let me guess: a soccer player!

Greg Well, that would be great, but I'm not that good. I want to be a designer.

Holly Really? What do you want to design?

Greg Clothes. Look, if you tell me about your company, I'll show you some of my designs.

Holly Hmm … I'll think about it.

Greg OK. You know, if this exhibition is right, there won't be any jobs for us, Holly. What if the robots take them all?

Holly I'm not sure they will, Greg. The exhibition's name is Robot Jobs, right? That means it has to show us the things that robots will do. But maybe jobs won't change very much.

Greg Let's hope you're right! Oh, look, Holly. This place is called the Orange Room. We can press buttons on the robots here. Let's go in!

 18

Hello, everyone. Thanks for coming to the Robot Jobs exhibition today, and welcome to the Orange Room! I'd like to show you one of the most interesting robots in our exhibition now. She's called the 28QAZ, but we prefer to call her Betty. You can program Betty to be many things. She's amazing! For example, you can ask her to be your home assistant. If you press the purple button, Betty will do all the daily tasks at home. That's right: you'll never have to wash or dry the dishes again! If you press the pink button, your robot will become an artist. You can ask her to paint anything you like, from people to places. Look! Betty paints so quickly, and isn't that beautiful? If you press the black button, Betty will become a mechanic. This means you'll never have to worry about your car. But what if you press the gray button? Let me show you. If you press the gray button, Betty will … Oh, no! What's happening? Hmm … It's not working. Oh, come on, Betty! No! It's turned off. No, no, don't go, everyone! Please, please, come back! It'll be OK in a minute …

Unit 9 page 82

 19

Eve Wow! Are you sure that this is a real ship, Dad?

Dad Of course! It's a museum now, but a long time ago, people sailed this ship around the world.

Eve That's amazing! Look, Dad. This is where the captain stood.

Dad That's right. The captain stood here.

Eve Imagine being a sailor and sailing this ship around the world. Months and months at sea. In the wind and rain. With rats on board, too! Argh!

Dad Ha ha! Not easy, Eve!

Eve What should we look at next?

Dad Well, we've already seen the cabins and looked through the portholes. Hmm … have we seen the old barometers yet?

Eve Yes, we have. We saw the old barometers at the beginning, remember?

Dad Oh, yes.

Eve I know! We haven't seen the lifeboats yet. Come on! Let's find them.

Dad Great idea. The lifeboats should be near the … Argh!

Eve What's wrong, Dad?

Dad I've just seen a rat!

Eve A rat? Where?

Dad There! Look—under the mast.

Eve OK, Dad. There is a rat under the mast. But it's made of plastic!

 20

Mom OK, I know it's boring, Robert. But I don't want to get on board and find out that we've forgotten something important. When we're in the middle of the ocean, it won't be so easy to buy things.

Robert But there will be stores on the ship, right, Mom?

Mom Well, there will be some stores on the ship, but it's better to bring the things that we need.

Robert OK, Mom.

Mom OK. Let's do a quick check, then. Have you packed your clothes yet?

Robert Of course I have! I packed my clothes first.

Mom Great. You've packed your clothes. What about books? Have you packed any books yet?

Robert Well, I haven't packed any books yet, but I've already put some ebooks on my phone.

Mom That's a good plan. Ebooks aren't heavy! Now, have you put your …

Robert Mom?

Mom Yes, Robert?

Robert Have you been on a ship before?

Mom Yes, I have. Your dad and I sailed around the South Pacific before you were born.

Robert That sounds exciting!

Mom It was. But Grandpa's the real sailor in the family. He was a sailor for twenty-five years.

Robert Wow! Twenty-five years is a long time! Where did he go?

Mom Oh, everywhere. He visited thirty-five countries. He took your dad on some of his trips, you know.

Robert That's amazing!

Mom OK, let's get back to the check. We've already talked about clothes and books. Now, what about …

Acknowledgments

The authors and publishers acknowledge the following sources of copyright material and are grateful for the permissions granted. While every effort has been made, it has not always been possible to identify the sources of all the material used, or to trace all copyright holders. If any omissions are brought to our notice, we will be happy to include the appropriate acknowledgments on reprinting and in the next update to the digital edition, as applicable.

Key: ST = Starter, U = Unit

Photography

The following images are sourced from Getty Images.

ST: Ableimages/DigitalVision; Universal History Archive/Universal Images Group; **U1**: Prof. Stewart Lowther/ Science Photo Library; monkeybusinessimages/iStock/Getty Images Plus; Claudiad/iStock/Getty Images Plus; shayes17/E+; Willoughby Owen/Moment; Ian McDonnell/E+; RicAguiar/iStock/Getty Images Plus; Bob Carey/The Image Bank/Getty Images Plus; Westend61; **U2**: Paul Souders/Stone/Getty Images Plus; SharonDay/iStock/Getty Images Plus; Morgan Paul/500px; Octávio Ferreira/EyeEm; Matt Stirn/Aurora Photos/ Panama; grass-lifeisgood/Moment; Westend61; Eduardo Fonseca Arraes/Moment; Michael J. Cohen/Moment Open; Danita Delimont/Gallo Images; Visuals Unlimited, Inc./Andres Morya/Visuals Unlimited; Ian Trower/ robertharding; Robert Seitz/imageBROKER; Rafal Cichawa/iStock/Getty Images Plus; **U3**: PeopleImages/ E+; THEPALMER/E+; gilaxia/E+; **U4**: PhonlamaiPhoto/iStock/Getty Images Plus; undefined undefined/iStock/ Getty Images Plus; Patrick Kawahara/EyeEm; JimDPhoto/E+; Nikada/iStock/Getty Images Plus; jax10289/ iStock/Getty Images Plus; lleerogers/iStock/Getty Images Plus; JGI/Jamie Grill/Blend Images; **U5**: bulentozber/ iStock/Getty Images Plus; Issaurinko/iStock/Getty Images Plus; chollacholla/iStock/Getty Images Plus; Firmafotografen/iStock/Getty Images Plus; LeventKonuk/iStock/Getty Images Plus; Siraphol/iStock/Getty Images Plus; **U6**: Edwin Remsberg/The Image Bank/Getty Images Plus; Chris McGrath/Getty Images News; fotostorm/iStock/Getty Images Plus; Sylvain Sonnet/Photolibrary; MarquesPhotography/iStock/Getty Images Plus; **U7**: Thorney Lieberman/Photographer's Choice/Getty Images Plus; JGI/Jamie Grill/Blend Images; Dennis K. Johnson/Lonely Planet Images; **U8**: Fanatic Studio; Rodolfo Arguedas/iStock/Getty Images Plus; **U9**: whitemay/E+; Fuse/Corbis; Zero Creatives/Cultura; JackF/iStock/Getty Images Plus; Allan Baxter/ The Image Bank.

The following images are sourced from other libraries.

U2: Johnny Lye/Thinkstock; **U8**: Zapp2Photo/Shutterstock.

Illustrations

Blooberry Design; Chris Chalik (Bright Agency); Sam Church; EMC Design Limited; Graham Kennedy; Daniel Limon (Beehive); Alan Rowe; Dave Smith (Beehive); Rupert Van Wyk (Beehive).

Audio

All the audio clips are sourced from Getty Images.

Allan Matsov/Sound Effects; Cedric Hommel/Sound Effects; Derridon/Sound Effects; John Scudder/Sound Effects; Jonny Slatter/Sound Effects; Sound Effects; Vitaliy Arkhanhelski/Sound Effects.

Audio produced by John Marshall Media.

Typeset

EMC Design Limited.

Cover design by We Are Bold.